My Contemporaries

Jean
Cocteau
1954

My Contemporaries

Jean Cocteau

Edited and introduced by Margaret Crosland

Chilton Book Company

Philadelphia   New York   London

848
C

Material used in this book is copyrighted as follows:

Portraits-Souvenir © 1935, Editions Bernard Grasset
Colette © 1955, Editions Bernard Grasset
La Corrida du Premier Mai © 1957, Editions Bernard Grasset
Essai de Critique Indirecte © 1959, Editions Bernard Grasset
Journal d'un Inconnu © 1952, Editions Bernard Grasset & Elek
    Books Ltd.
André Gide © 1951, *Nouvelle Revue Française*
Modigliani © 1950, Ferdinand Hazan
Raymond Radiguet © 1943, Radio Nationale
Au Bal du la Chance © 1958, Editions Jeheber
Maalesh © 1950, Editions Gallimard
Mon Premier Voyage © 1937, Editions Gallimard
Le Cordon Ombilical © 1962, Plou (Librairie)
Opium © 1957, Peter Owen/Librairie Stock
Masques et Visages © 1951, Calmann-Levy
All other material © 1967, Peter Owen Ltd. and © 1968, Chilton
    Book Company.
The self-portrait of Jean Cocteau, originally drawn for Margaret
Crosland's biography, is reproduced by courtesy of Mrs. Susi
Mautner.

First Edition   *All rights reserved*
Published in Philadelphia, 1968, by Chilton Book Company
Library of Congress Catalog Card Number 68-31695
Designed by Warren Infield
Manufactured in the United States of America
by Quinn & Boden Company, Inc., Rahway, N. J.

Contents

Introduction

Jean Cocteau, who died in 1963, was published continuously all his life from 1918 onwards (he wanted three earlier collections of poems excluded from the "official" bibliography) and several titles have appeared since his death. As a result the list of his complete works, classified, in accordance with his own system, into different branches of Poésie, *including* Poésie du Roman *and* Poésie du Cinéma, *fills many pages. Anyone interested in twentieth-century French literature, or the international theater and cinema, can hardly avoid Cocteau—his shadow falls across every path, his voice is heard in every conversation.*

Among those who know his work, some will acquire their favorite pieces and remain faithful to them, while others will occasionally make experiments, even if they continually go on looking for what they already know and like. Most people who have seen one of his films or read one of his novels will usually want to see and read further, but they often find difficulty in knowing where to begin; it can also happen that one work which confuses or disappoints them will remove their appetite for more. This would be a pity, for so many assessments of Cocteau, so much anger and mere ignorance, so many dismissals, are caused because his work has not been sufficiently absorbed. When I first saw the film Orphée *I was impatient with it; when I saw it the second time I had read most of Cocteau's books and I realized what* Orphée *was about. Since then it has meant more to me each time I have seen it; I made a point of seeing his first film,* Le Sang d'un Poète *and I began to find cross-references throughout his work which I had not suspected before.*

The first difficulty for the uninitiated is that the work seems to be unlike that of any other writer who is either acknowledged to be major or at least controversial. It does not conform: much of it has no orthodox intellectual content, it does not appear to "say" anything in the accepted sense, and the usual implications of intellectuality do not seem to apply at all. The newcomer immediately asks: what is it all about? A good question, obviously, and one which cannot be answered in entirety here. Indirectly it is all about Cocteau, much of it obviously and subjectively so, all about a man who worked as a creative artist in an astonishingly, perhaps dangerously large number of fields: who wrote poetry, novels, plays and essays, drew and painted on a small and large scale, made films, devised ballets. Although this vast body of work can be compartmented to a certain extent the average intellectual, who is supremely conformist, distrusts so much diversity and speed, is baffled by Cocteau's failure to proceed at a regular pace along a straight line and is inclined to be jealous or impatient about work which has attracted such a mixed and indefinable public.

Cocteau always worked in his own way, he has never belonged to any obvious school and has defied any label. Sometimes he appeared to be ahead of his time, sometimes an exact contemporary, dans le vent but not avant-garde, and occasionally he would baffle everyone by writing a piece, the play Les Parents Terribles, for instance, that appeared on the surface "commercial" and even old-fashioned. He condemned La Machine à Ecrire himself, and if L'Aigle à Deux Têtes is a possible play, it was a bad film. In spite of his long writing life there was little "development" of the orthodox type. However much he absorbed and learned during a perpetually creative lifetime, his approach was always instinctive and individualistic to such an extent that one feels he was born and lived all his life being, knowing and saying the same things. Only the means of expression, the emphasis and orientation vary, due to influences of different kinds, usually the thought, technique or works of other people. As he grew older his voice became perhaps sadder, but it never changed.

His detractors have often pointed out a tendency to repeat himself over and again, a tendency which they regard as inseparable from a paucity of ideas.

Not only his detractors say this, but his admirers also, for it is true, and there is a reason for it. The subjectivity and in-

dividualism of Cocteau's work have rarely been isolationist, and the most personal aspects have rarely been limited to the egocentric I. Part of his individualism has always lain in his receptivity, his capacity for expressing ideas and feelings through some kind of contact with other minds, relationships of all types. One aspect of his genius was a talent for creative friendship, a love of loving as apart from love. "I have said somewhere that I was better at making friends than at making love. Love is based on brief spasms . . . friendship is a quiet spasm." As I see it, one of the most interesting aspects of his personality was his capacity for expressing ideas and feelings through relationships of all kinds, and these relationships in his case are inevitably friendly and constructive ones. A talent for friendship implies that friendship endures, for a true friend does not change. It is only the fact of living longer that leads us to say different things to or about our friends. Basically we keep on saying the same thing. There may be modulation, but the changes of key are closely related and establish their own pattern of unity.

The themes in Cocteau's work—theme is a more appropriate word than idea—are like his friends; he keeps them all his life, and most of them are inherent in the people he admired and loved. It is important that the word "friendship" should not be interpreted only as a close personal relationship: for Cocteau had friendship not only for Radiguet or Picasso but for authors or thinkers long dead, or people he admired from a distance when very young, or even people who actively disliked him. He also felt friendship for an object or an abstraction because he established a two-way relationship with any theme about which he wrote. He analyzed as a friend would do, seeing everything in the round. He was incapable of writing about a painting, for instance, as though he were standing squarely in front of it and recapitulating the painter's development, past, present and future, in chronological order: that is for the art critic or historian.

This method of writing appreciative criticism—such terminology can only be approximate and is certainly limited—is an extension of the way he wrote about his friends or people with whom he established some lasting contact. It seems vital therefore to realize that the essence of his work can be found first of all in his portraits of people, for they illustrate everything in it that is accessible, sympathetic, memorable, durable, all-pervading or merely dazzling. He has said more than once that from his point of view writing and drawing were not really different—they were merely different ways of tying the lines together. Through his descriptions of people we can see many aspects of his genius: first, the skill in selecting and translating his observation, through brilliant handling of words, into a verbal portrait or a caricature, sometimes enhanced by actual drawings, sometimes standing alone. Occasionally he can make a person more tangible still through the incredibly evocative atmosphere of his background: such as Proust in his cork-lined bedroom.

In some cases a "portrait" by Cocteau is mainly visual, although his use of visual description never stops short and never produces a static result, for his subjects invariably move and talk. It is important to remember that with Cocteau everything is theatrical: his first impressions were so closely linked with the theater that for him ordinary life has always appeared a statement in dramatic terms. He did not falsify it, he saw it that way, and he was intensely selective. Historical personages, like the Empress Eugénie, become retired actresses; sometimes the "characters" seem not so much to talk as to say their lines, like the Comtesse de Noailles. Yet even the most apparently simple of the portraits express what the "subjects" felt and thought, how Cocteau reacted to them, and how he felt himself being influenced, probably for life.

Although it is impossible and unnecessary to generalize about Cocteau, one other general aspect emerges from a study of these portraits: the fact that as an essentially creative man he liked creative people. He would search out the creativity in anyone he liked. He never separated men or women from their work (which was not necessarily productive and was sometimes, as in the case of an actor or actress, a creative, dramatic or merely eccentric way of life), for he himself did not divide life and work into two compartments; a man is his life and lives his work.

In selecting the descriptions that Cocteau made of his contemporaries I have omitted some people who occupied a place in his private mythology, Jacques Maritain and Jean Desbordes, for instance, either because the passages about them do not easily fit into the "portrait" framework which he adopted in so many other cases, or else because they are too little known or appreciated outside France. Many striking portraits of Cocteau's friends are of course included in La Difficulté d'Etre, *which was published in France in 1947 and is a key book in every aspect of Cocteau's development. In many of the portraits quoted I have referred the reader to passages in other books which are complementary in some way to those I have chosen for this anthology. The only "person" I have excluded with regret is the schoolboy Dargelos, vital and lasting symbol though he is in Cocteau's work. Some biographers have carried out detailed research, without much success, into his material existence, but I feel his personality is more like a penetrating essence, and in this gallery of more tangible portraits I believe it would be out of place to quote any of the more specific passages about him. It is perhaps significant that although there is a file at the Lycée Condorcet in Paris (where he was at school with Cocteau) stating that Dargelos was born at Agen in the Southwest, there is no trace in the municipal records at Agen to show that anyone of that name lived there at the relevant time. I have been more preoccupied in this book with the transmutation of the real into the legendary than with the reverse process, and this discovery—by Monsieur Jean-Jacques Khim[1]—has reinforced my decision.*

I hope that the portrait gallery which follows, presenting as it does Cocteau's contemporaries over a span of fifty years, will provide an introduction to his work and allow caricature, impressions and studies to be enjoyed for their own sake, while at the same time the reader can identify some elements for a self-portrait of Cocteau. If his work should sometimes seem an endless corridor with many minor passages leading off into some impenetrable labyrinth, his evocative descriptions of people are like brightly illuminated patches glowing on the walls; going from one to another we suddenly realize, without noticing the fact, that we have moved along the corridor, learning something of the way that poets walk, slightly above the ground. We are not expected

[1] *Cocteau*, Jean-Jacques Khim, Paris, 1960.

Introduction

*to walk between mysteriously billowing curtains, like Beauty in
La Belle et la Bête, we are no longer bemused by unidentified
hands holding candelabra to light our way: we meet instead real
faces, real people, and even Cocteau himself.*

*Except where indicated in the introductory passages, the trans-
lations are my own.*

Margaret Crosland

My Contemporaries

Edouard de Max

In the 1930's Cocteau was persuaded to write for the Paris news-paper Le Figaro a series of articles, accompanied by drawings, about his family life when young and about famous people he had known, admired, worked with, at the turn of the century and soon afterwards. The results were so entertaining and successful that in 1935 they were published in book form as Portraits-Souvenir, the title based on "the sort of costume found in the booths of fair-ground photographers. The customer puts his head through a huge painted collar and is uprooted, transported behind an airplane pro-peller or flung into a Serpollet car or a boxing ring." However, Cocteau did not intend merely to transplant this technique into words: "The souvenir portraits I would like to take are different—the customer must create his own reality and prevent me from confusing dates and backgrounds, a confusion which is the essence of those amusing fairground pictures but which hardly contributes to my search for exactness."

He described the dignified eccentricity of his family and their friends and devoted a large part of the book to the great enter-tainers, or "sacred monsters," as he called them, figures who in-fluenced him, sometimes helped him and were at least partly responsible for his way of seeing life, creative work and the world generally in theatrical terms.

The portrait of Edouard de Max is one of the most memorable in the collection and "fixes" the whole era of the great ham actors. The name of De Max has never been a household word with the magical ring of "Isadora Duncan" or "Sir Henry Irving," but this does not matter: Cocteau's way of describing him brings to life a whole period, a moment in social history which has now receded just far enough to earn our somewhat envious wonderment.

de Max

Jean

. . . Sarah (Bernhardt) and de Max often acted together, opposite the Châtelet.[1] . . .

What excitement when the yellow curtain parted at the end of the play, and the tragedienne bowed, the claws of her left hand embedded in her right breast, her right hand at the end of her straight arm resting on the edge of the proscenium. Like some Venetian palace she sank beneath the weight of necklaces and fatigue, painted, gilded, engineered, propped up and hung with flags, in the midst of a dovecote of applause. *La Sorcière! La Samaritaine! Phèdre! Andromaque!* . . . Hermione rests in her dressing-room. Orestes goes mad. *"Pour qui sont—ces serpents—qui sifflent—sur—vos têtes."* De Max panted, shaking his serpent-like locks and waving draperies about like Loie Fuller. A kind of poignant lament accompanied him, which for a long time we took for some sound in the wings and was nothing more than the siren of the paddle steamer at the Châtelet landing-stage.

De Max was a tragedian of genius. Like Mesdames Duncan and Bernhardt, he was ignorant of codes and formulas. He searched and invented. He embarrassed. He went off the rails. We felt as though we were responsible for his mistakes. We did not dare look at our neighbors; we sweated hotly. Suddenly we were ashamed of being ashamed. Shouts of "quiet" suppressed the last laugh. With a raging fist de Max tamed ridicule and leaped astride it. His pride carried him away and carried us away at a gallop.

How can I forget his Néron in *Britannicus*, an operetta Néron, with an emerald monocle and a train, played in such a way that it made you unable to imagine any other? . . .

Like the sea, whose motion, sound and glaucous coloring he possessed, de Max's name spelled terror to any mother. (Except mine, who trusted me and was perfect.) "Your son knows de Max, he's ruined." This was their *leitmotiv*, and it was inaccuracy itself. There were no black masses, or rosy ones. There were no traps for young men. De Max's private life was more like the family circle of a caravanful of gipsies, and his bedroom was like that of Louis

[1] A theater where Cocteau saw many exciting melodramas when he was a boy.

XIV. He received his courtiers, his male favorites and his female favorites—the latter, a real harem of delightful women.

From my first visit I still have a photograph with the dedication: *A vos seize ans en fleur, mes quarante en pleurs,* and the memory of a curious dedication from Mounet-Sully[2] which adorned the bedroom: *A de Max son admirateur admirable.* De Max was as ageless as a cat. Chieftain, Emir, large Siamese, or black panther, he would curl up in the semi-darkness among the dirty cushions and furs where our sharp eyes recognized the costume of Hippolyte.[3]

Much later I was to know the bric-a-brac at the Marquise Casati's. I prefer her unicorn's horn, stuffed boas, bronze hinds and mechanical tigers to the nice little audacities of fashion and that good taste which puts yesterday's bad taste on a pedestal and radiates nothing mysterious or significant. A room resembles its occupant. It is the soul's costume, a costume which our soul alters and to which it quickly gives shape. Once it is imposed on the soul a room shapes our behavior. Tidiness and untidiness do not imitate each other. . . .

With de Max untidiness was his style, his acting, the caprices of a warm, generous and oriental nature. In this apartment that was feared and laughed at and formed his being, the examples we received were those of nobility only.

Marie, the elderly maid with Guanhumarah's gray hair, opened the door to the vestibule. The guest went through a series of rooms which owed something to the Fratellinis'[4] dressing-room, a taxidermist's shop and the workroom of Coppelius or Faust. On a pale green upright piano carved with climbing pink roses, were stacks of books—Verlaine, Baudelaire, Verhaeren and Gide—bound as heavily as prayer books. You had to pick your way through the fluted columns, Gothic chests and cathedral tapers. Four steps led down to the pseudo-Pompeian bathroom; to the right a bay win-

[2] Well-known tragic actor, 1841–1916.

[3] In Racine's play, the son of Thésée, with whom Phèdre is in love.

[4] The famous clowns whom Cocteau admired greatly. He devised the farcical ballet *Le Boeuf sur le Toit* in 1920 with roles for all three brothers.

Jean
Sarah

dow looked on to a dismal little Paris garden. A dead hosepipe, a dead lawn and prison walls. An archway separated the bedroom from the writing table. De Max dipped his pen in the mouth of a pottery toad. He wrote in violet ink in tall spiky handwriting, which he dried with gold dust. He kept his money in a little cup and distributed it to anyone poorer than himself.

If he went out he donned a pearl-gray corduroy velvet suit, fastened a pearl-gray tiepin in his black satin cravat, fixed the big gray pearl-shaped bowler hat over his left ear, put on pearl-gray gloves, dabbed pearly powder over his gray double chin, moistened his yellow-rimmed eyes with saliva, and in his little patent-leather boots with their pearl-gray uppers he went out, crossed the court-yard, climbed into his pearl-gray "electric" and there, sitting stiffly upright, revealing to numismatists the coins of his two profiles, he drove in silence towards the Bois de Boulogne. Motionless, he drove around the lake, gazing heavenwards, with a beauty spot at the corner of his nostril and a bitter twist to his mouth, and re-turned by the same route. In the evening he interpreted plays in eight acts by Ferdinand Hérold and Paul Vérola: *Bouddha, Ramsès II* and goodness knows what others—all the heroes and all the legends which stimulated his craze for costumes and attitudes.

Light reading it may be, but this baroque portrait illustrates per-fectly what Cocteau meant in his preface to this book when he wrote of the "sacred monsters": "the originality of their appearance (which distinguished them from others, threw them into relief and made them into personalities) arose not so much from a desire to stand out, but from a struggle with death. . . ." Without Cocteau's portrait of him, Edouard de Max might not have survived. And the younger man was quick to acknowledge his more practical debt to the old actor:

He organized a reading at the Théâtre Fémina devoted to my poems and paid for it out of his own pocket. The most famous actresses came at his request. . . . It is nonetheless true that my beginnings date from that reading and that the efforts I had to make afterwards to have it forgotten were enough to make it un-forgettable. But in the end de Max helped me. He read deeper than my silly poems and guessed there was a hidden strength within me, forcing me to conquer myself and teaching me that greatness does not easily go hand in hand with delicate nuances.

Catulle Mendès

This second outstanding portrait from the same collection uses the same virtuoso technique and omits nearly all the reference book facts: Cocteau is not concerned with telling his readers that Catulle Mendès, who was of Jewish origin, was born in Bordeaux in 1841 and when he was only twenty was imprisoned and fined for the licentious Roman d'une Nuit, *published in the* Revue Fantaisiste *which he had founded himself. He wrote Parnassian poetry, plays and novels much greater in quantity than in quality, made a suitable but short-lived marriage to Judith Gautier, younger daughter of the famous poet; her poetry was better than her husband's, but some of Catulle Mendès' critical appraisals can still be read with profit. Although he was a highly influential critic and editor when Cocteau was a young man, the author of* Portraits-Souvenir *saw him, as he saw a great many people, as an actor, a "sacred monster."*

Cocteau softens his subject's absurdities with a cloud of gentle laughter, and his apologies for having been unkind to him in the past are worth noting, for the later writing frequently revealed Cocteau's horror of any attitude that was not constructive and expressive of love. . . . "I love loving," he wrote in La Difficulté d'Etre, *"I hate hatred." He regarded this as the secret of his happiness.*

Although this description and the one that follows have all the memorable features of a true portrait, they are in one way moving pictures; perhaps it was Cocteau's passion for circus performers that made him so interested in speed and all types of movement as well as precarious balance. As a result we see and remember Catulle Mendès moving with his strange gait down the theater corridor, close to everyone but at the same time immensely far away.

6

Jean

Catulle
mendès.

The blind man belongs to tragedy, the deaf man to comedy. You will never make anyone laugh at a blind husband (in the literal sense), and you will never move them with a deaf one. And yet the deaf are more closed in, more excluded from the world than the blind, and they are sadder. There are blind men who are gay, blind men who enjoy themselves; but the deaf man is incurably sad. If you think about it, it is not difficult to recall the past with one's eyes. It is another matter to do so with one's ears. We can easily imagine the setting for a dinner given by Louis XIV; but the sound of voices, the way of talking, joking and laughing escape us. We can imagine a square in Athens on a festival day and the ladies arriving at the theater at cock-crow, at six o'clock in the morning, for the *première* of *Antigone*; but it is impossible to invent the sound of it. The future will probe this emptiness and will discover fragments of fanfares, the chatter of crowds and the declamation of orators. The silence of the past weighs heavily upon us and the music of the Greeks remains a mystery.

If the lines of the drawings which accompany this chapter surprise you, you must realize that I am not using any caricatures made at the time; I am drawing from memory, trying to use my writing pen and my drawing pen in the same rhythm. It is not easy. And when I hesitate, when the faces of which I speak remain only a misty likeness, I try to obtain one characteristic which corresponds to my memory. A pen is so ineffective. A sketch is so little. I would like to be able to convey to you the sound of dead voices, to break open this unbearable tomb of sound, to wrest something more than silhouettes from vanished years and by some unimaginable trick let you hear the ha-ha-ha with which Catulle Mendès accompanied the slightest sentence, the muffled voice of Edmond Rostand or the laughter which Proust smeared over his face with his white-gloved hand and his beard.

I knew Catulle Mendès a little before the Théâtre Fémina reading organized by de Max (whom my uncle Raymond Lecomte, who despised "mountebanks" and respected the correct use of the preposition, insisted on calling "the actor Max"). Mendès seemed to him beyond the pale, and he forced my family to share this verdict. I admired Mendès in secret therefore, and did not dare confess an item of news which was to subject my nerves to a severe ordeal; Catulle Mendès, after the Fémina reading, had invited me to luncheon at his home in the boulevard Malesherbes. Keeping this event to myself and waiting for the date almost made me ill. At last the day arrived. And first of all I must try to describe the critic of *Le Journal*, who was feared by the playwrights, was a playwright himself and a poet less read than celebrated.

During that long hateful period when youth seeks out the last word in refinement and turns against its masters, I happened to laugh at Catulle Mendès and described him without love. I regret it. May his shade find my apologies here. In what better way could I offer them to him, and how could I pay him homage better than in these souvenir portraits, where I concentrate on visual memories, purposely setting aside those intimate memories which assail us at the moment of our death?

The palisade of Greta Garbo's eyelashes, the dresses worn by Marlene Dietrich in the Shanghai express and the young men's clothes which these artists wear in private life certainly create a new romanticism. But the sacred monsters of flesh and blood are dying out, and I believe young people nowadays will never again see the likes of such as Catulle Mendès and his wife, or Ernest La Jeunesse or Jean de Bonnefon, his head adorned with thousands of little gray curls like frills.

Catulle Mendès in the theater corridor during the interval! I hardly dare undertake this description, and first of all I must warn you about the danger of confusing emphasis with caricature, and the blackness of an etching with the blackness of the heart. I would like everyone to understand the admiring respect with which I approach a defunct figure who trailed behind him the august ruins of Romanticism and the purple of its gods.

Catulle Mendès was fat and walked lightly. His hips and shoulders undulated. A kind of airship roll propelled him blindly along. The crowd parted in surprise as he passed. He was like a lion and a turbot. His cheeks, eyes and little fish-like half-moon mouth seemed to be imprisoned in some sort of jelly which kept him at a distance and put some mysterious transparent trembling layer between him and the rest of the world. He had the same little curls, waves and reddish moustache as a lion, the same proud mane and the same tail, formed by the tails of his black dress suit hanging down below the short putty-colored coat which was left untidily open. His coat carried the red ribbon of the Legion of Honor and revealed his loose white cravat, his shirt-front stained with coffee, his jacket, his shirt showing between his dress-waistcoat and his trousers which hung in countless folds over tiny pointed boots. In his charming pale plump hand he carried a Chaplinesque walking stick.

And so, with his opera hat upside down, his plaster-cast eyes, his curls hanging down on his high narrow shoulders, his elbows by his side and his cuffs sticking out of his sleeves, Catulle Mendès, the terrible trustee of tomorrow's oracles, followed his corporation, a magnificent and prow-like figure cutting his way through the waves of spectators. He was escorted by Madame Mendès, who was tall, as painted as an idol, and behind the aquarium of her draperies, followed by the frothing folds of her mandarin sleeves and trains, looked like some marvelous Japanese fish.

De Max led me towards the couple. Mendès and his wife stopped in the midst of the ebbing tide. De Max introduced me, his illustrious voice penetrating those thick layers which made Mendès inaccessible to timid people, and it was then that Mendès said to me with his inimitable ha-ha-ha, "Young man, come and share my omelette next Wednesday."

You can imagine that on Wednesday I could hardly contain myself and arrived early. I rang. A maid opened the door and asked me what I wanted. More dead than alive, I murmured that I had come to luncheon, that the master had invited me. The maid let me keep my hat and pushed me into a dark room. Gradually objects emerged from the gloom. Simple Chinese furniture, an artistic bronze on the chimney-piece. Between the window and the chimney-piece, a marvelous portrait: Banville by Renoir.

I waited. I waited. At last a door slammed. A discussion . . . and the horrible conviction that Mendès had come home and had forgotten me. It was too late to escape. I still remained alone for a long time. All at once a door that I had not been watching opened, and Mendès appeared, most strangely, for he wore a mask, a real carnival mask with a lace border. He made his apologies, admitted that he had forgotten me, but said that I should share his luncheon, and explained that he had had a fall the day before on the boulevard Malesherbes. The mask was to keep in place a plaster on his nose.

We went to the table. Both in Paris and Saint-Germain (his country house), Mendès adorned his dining-room with an aviary. He was mad about birds, which he collected and called by their names. The birds flew out of their cages, fluttering round the sideboards, chirping and pecking crumbs off the tablecloth.

The German chemist Schliemann paid for the luxury of opening up the tombs of Mycene and seeing the Atrides, who were buried standing up, wearing their golden masks. He had barely enjoyed this costly spectacle when the great corpses vanished into dust. And so, through contact with this man who opened up as the bottles emptied, I saw the great shades of Baudelaire, de Nerval, Rimbaud, Verlaine. Alas, like the Atrides, they now consisted only of a golden powder, a mist which left their outlines to the imagination. No matter, I shall never forget that luncheon, that omelette, the ha-ha-ha of the master as he spoke and gesticulated, interpolating dates and anecdotes, yet bringing out of his confused memory a procession of dead kings.

Afterwards I was to lunch with Catulle Mendès every Saturday at Saint-Germain, with the same birds and the same verbal resurrections. At four o'clock Mendès got ready, injected drugs into his eyes and into his thighs through his clothes and yelled as he sprayed himself with Pennès vinegar. Once in motion, he took the train and did not stop again before reaching the *terrasse* of a boulevard café.

His death astounded me. The news was given to me over the telephone by his maid. After dining with his friends the Oppenheims, where he had drunk nothing because of some injury to his pride, he returned in an abnormal state and mistook the tunnel and its lamps for the darkness of the station platform. He fell down and the trains crushed him to death.

I went to the Hôtel Meurice to announce the tragedy to the Rostands. I had become very friendly with Maurice, who with François Bernouard and I had founded a magazine called *Schéhéra-*

zade, with a cover that represented a naked Sultana by Iribe, and it was quite simply the first luxury review devoted entirely to poets. Maurice and I were the young men of the moment. The era of young men, which was inaugurated by Raymond Radiguet, did not yet exist. We believed we were Byron and Shelley and that this could be achieved merely by talking about Oxford and going down the Champs-Elysées in an open carriage in the April sunshine.

At Saint-Germain a crowd of people invaded the garden and the vestibule. Mendès rested in a little room reserved for the Larousse. Léon Dierx wept. A sheet concealed the mutilated body and the wax tapers illuminated an admirably beautiful face. The face of a dead man returns to the contours of adolescence. The death mask of Napoleon from Saint Helena reveals the cheek-bones and profile of Bonaparte. In death Mendès looked like Heine, and I remembered a story that I had heard him tell: when he was young he went to see Heine's widow and she collapsed, fainting, for the resemblance was so strong that she believed her crippled husband had found his legs again and walked.

Anna de Noailles

Cocteau's description of the Comtesse de Noailles, inseparable from the amusing yet touching sketches which accompany it, is a minor masterpiece; a straightforward description of the remarkable woman whose father was a Roumanian prince and her mother a musically gifted Greek would inevitably be flat, for nobody would ever believe in her. Yet this was how she lived (from 1876 to 1933) and talked; the only other writer to my knowledge who has succeeded in transmitting something of her insubstantial essence to paper is Maurice Goudeket, who describes an amusing encounter with her—in which he paid her back in her own coin—in his book La Douceur de Vieillir.

Few people read her poems nowadays, although they are deeply musical, show an excellent sense of form and in fact are much better than one might have imagined. She was the first Frenchwoman to be made a Commander of the Legion of Honor in 1931 and was also a member of the Royal Academy of French Language and Literature in Brussels. The memory of her friendship was so meaningful to Cocteau that in 1962 he planned what was to be his last book for a French publisher: La Comtesse de Noailles Oui et Non, *eventually published in 1963. The chapter from* Portraits-Souvenir *was reprinted in it, with references to the approval of Maurice Barrès and the disapproval of André Gide.*

The enduring friendship between Cocteau and the Comtesse illustrates the remarkable ease with which he moved in all kinds of society; unlike so many successful writers he saw no reason to despise the aristocracy, even those members of it who wrote poetry.

Again there is movement and animation throughout the whole description; and somehow one can hear the gentle clatter of the necklaces falling to the floor, a proof that it is not in fact too difficult, as Cocteau alleged in the portrait of Catulle Mendès, "to recall the past with one's ears."

Simone introduced me to Anna de Noailles in a car. She was coming away from some lecture or other. At first sight I admit she astounded me. The Comtesse was used to shining, playing a part and performing exercises that had become famous, and thanks to the credit which I enjoyed through Simone, she treated me, without the slightest preliminary, to a display which was a matter of course to her intimate friends but which was enough to make any new spectator feel like a provincial.

I must have looked like a frock-coated Fratellini beneath a shower of hats in the midst of one of those scenes of carnage which leave the circus ring strewn with old guitars, broken furniture, soap lather, saucepans and broken china.

Gradually I became used to it. The beauty of this little person and the graceful timbre of her voice, combined with an extraordinarily amusing power of description, triumphed over everything else, and I understood once and for all that her way of sniffing, leaning back, crossing her legs, stopping, opening her hands and flinging them away from herself as though from a sling, the gestures which strewed the floor with veils, scarves, necklaces, Arabian beads, muffs, handkerchiefs, miniature umbrellas, belts and safety pins, constituted her *décor*, her driving-power and in some way the props for her act.

I admit that as soon as I felt developing between us one of those friendships that last beyond the grave, I surrounded myself with all imaginable precautions. At table she wanted all the guests to listen to her and remain silent. I have quoted earlier that remark of Baudelaire's: "Hugo plunges into one of those monologues that he calls conversation." The Comtesse, even before going to eat, seized on a conversation of this type and would not let it go. If she drank she would hold her glass in her right hand and made a sign with her left that she must not be interrupted. And the guests obeyed. Hostesses "offered" her and repeated the *leitmotiv* "Anna is wonderful! Wonderful!" The Comtesse went on. Going from her maid to George Sand, from her valet to

Anne parle

Shakespeare, she juggled, walked up and down the tightrope, changed from one trapeze to another and performed conjuring tricks. Let us admit, and it is here that my precautions begin, she sometimes cheated, lifting cardboard weights and falling off the wire. Some did not notice, some laughed in their sleeves, and others suffered. I was among the latter. I pitied her, I saw her getting into difficulties, becoming muddled and taking short cuts. Anything rather than return to silence! A sort of madness of the tongue, some verbal vertigo prevented her from realizing her folly. After several experiences (sometimes she succeeded and did not slip), I decided that I would never meet her in public and would only see her tête-à-tête.

And yet . . . and yet. . . . Since I am letting myself go and proving my brotherly love by giving up the detestable habit of praise which, when it is taken too far, can cause a great deal of harm, I remember one evening that was profoundly successful. It was at the Princesse de Polignac's house. I liked the Princesse. I liked her way of coyly grinding out irrevocable judgments, accompanying them with a veiled smile and wagging her head like a malicious young elephant, I liked her magnificent profile, like a rock worn away by the sea. And it was certainly because the evening ended at her house that we had the good fortune to see Anna de Noailles in full possession of her faculties.

The evening was coming to a close. On the light-colored Savonnerie carpet, the music stands and the listeners' chairs stood about untidily. All at once, among this musical wreckage, I saw the Comtesse de Noailles sitting surrounded by a group of ladies. She was devoting herself to extraordinary exercises. The nightingale practices before the singing season. He caws, croaks, lows and squeaks, and those who are not aware of his methods are amazed, as they stand at the foot of the night-dark tree. The Comtesse began in the same way. I watched her from a distance. She sniffed, sneezed, burst out laughing, heaved heart-rending sighs and dropped Turkish necklaces and scarves. Then she took a deep breath, and, curling and uncurling her lips at full speed, she began. What did she say? I no longer know. I know that she talked and talked and talked and the big room filled with a crowd of people and the young ones sat on the floor and the older ones sat in armchairs around her. I know that the Princesse de Polignac and the Princesse de Caraman-Chimay (her friend and her sister), standing on her left and her right, seemed to be seconds in some dreamland boxing ring. I know that the servants in their black suits and the footmen in knee-breeches and powdered wigs came closer to the half-open doors. I know that through the open windows of June, like the waltz in a film by Lubitsch or in that film where Liszt played the piano, the words of the Comtesse bewitched the trees, the plants and the stars—that her words penetrated into the neighboring buildings, interrupted quarrels, enriched sleep, and that everything and everyone, from the star to the tree, from the tree to the chauffeurs of the waiting limousines, murmured "The Comtesse is talking . . . the Comtesse is talking . . . the Comtesse is talking. . . ."

Poor dear proud creature! She would have suffered too much from our rapid, disrespectful and inattentive era. Could even Wilde have devised an apologia for it? I doubt it. "Once upon a time. . . ." Everyone turns away. Conversations begin again. Gossip starts off-beat. Elbows jostle against one another. Legs touch, Wilde stops short, alone and haggard, with a crimson carnation in his hand.

What is more, I have been told that the Comtesse was the victim, during her last months, of just such a lack of appreciation. At the house of F.M., at the head of a tea table surrounded by elegant young women, she had tried to take the reins. A complete waste. The silly young creatures interrupted her right in the middle of a sentence, laughed at her, treating her (no more, no less) like a gambler at Monte Carlo.

The Comtesse grew smaller, pale and hollow-cheeked, like those Chinese nightingales which fall down flat at the bottom of their cages with their wings outstretched and die of an apoplectic fit.

Once more I was to see the Comtesse in public and in form. She had to meet Francis Jammes[1] at Madame Alphonse Daudet's house in the rue de Bellechasse. Jammes was coming to spend a

[1] The poet and novelist (1868–1938) who is remembered mostly for his writing about animals and country life.

week in Paris. He wore a snuff-colored suit, a red tie and beige spats. With his beard floating in the wind, his spectacles set for battle and his cheeks bulging, this superb vermeil triton navigated from group to group with an escort of young spiritualists, sounding an astonishing nasal trumpet. The Comtesse entered. Leaning backwards, wearing a poppy-trimmed straw hat, she stretched out her hands and inspected Jammes. He took hold of her little hands, bent down over the straw hat and repeated, "The great lady! Here is the great lady!"

Some of Jammes' poems were recited. He shuddered like a horse shooing flies away, waggled his thigh like an examiner and, with one leg crossed over the other, shook his pale-gloved foot like a hand. The Comtesse whispered to me: "Just look! The vet who has cured a human being!" And a few days later (I had asked her for a description of Jammes' visit), "We talked about the weather. It was no change from our books."

She fired these cracks like a machine gun. Nobody could aim better. Provided the spectators did not upset her and make her disastrously dizzy, she scored a bull's eye each time. Egg or eagle, she never missed. And after shooting down the eagle you could expect her to say, like the Austrian archduke, "What, has it only one head?" For this intuitive woman imagined she had the culture of a Goethe. The astonishing electricity that escaped from her, the lightning that played about her, the waves that emanated from her, she persisted in taking all this for intelligence. As for the naïveté of genius, she would have none of it. Madame de Montebello's remark, "Anna looks at Versailles with the eyes of Zamore," disgusted her. This disgust formed the theme of long intimate sessions "behind the curtains"; this was the expression which described our custom of avoiding each other outside and of meeting only at her house, 40 rue Scheffer.

Ginet, the old servant, stank of the cellar. He propelled me in zigzags towards a padded door, which opened into a little room of silence, the end of a corridor which intercepted sounds; the walls were lined with books and cork, and the carpets rested on cotton-wool. This dark silence preceded a second padded door. The bedroom door. I would go in. Anna de Noailles received her guests reclining on a wide Louis XV bed. The room was that of a young girl in about 1900. The only contrast was an enlarged photograph of Minerva, her forehead resting against her lance. Leaning stiffly to one side, helmet on head, like a figure seven, she stood in meditation. But this pensive Minerva was not Anna's patron; hers was more likely to be the turbulent Pallas of the *Aeneid*, the grasshopper from the Acropolis, the sacred hill from where the Musurus tribe brought her down. Indeed it was not Anna, this little leaning-column Minerva. It was not she whom Maurras would embrace in the Parthenon. Maurras classes the young countess-poet with the *"magots,"* those primitive ladies in the Acropolis museum who recline on their tombs, their smiling faces consumed by their eyes, beside their bearded husbands. What a contrast—like that between the bedroom and Minerva—between these yellow ribbons, laces, cretonnes, the furniture with twisted legs, these trinkets of all types and the lady of the house! Her raven-wing hair, a catogan and a long tress (she called it her Colonne Vendôme) descending in spirals over her shoulders, and her large eyeballs looking as though they were painted on a band covering her eyes so that she had to raise her head to look out from underneath. These artificial eyes, these huge eyes, streamed out right and left from her horizontal face. A strong nose, like a beak, and deep-cut nostrils powerful enough to breathe in all the scents in the world. The graceful mouth, with lips curling like rose petals, revealed the jaws of a carnivore. This framework and animal-like bone structure illustrated the remark of Lemaître. What a delightful insect! The microscope reveals an arsenal of saws, pincers and antennae.

Why did her death remind me of the sublime death of the scorpion who thrusts a dagger into itself, surrounded by flames?

Born for the grass and for "a rose tree to spring from her bones," born to be dead, she could not bear the glowing bonfire of the old world and its threatening flames. She was weary.

She liked crimson, the sign of power. This woman who loved Jaurès suspended the saber of Mangin at the foot of her bed.

It was fame that she worshipped. Fame, her *idée fixe*! "You only admire second-raters," she said to me. In vain did I demonstrate to her that the privilege of France was precisely the possession of secret glories, famous men of whom the mass know nothing. Rimbaud is hardly known. Verlaine only just. Hugo's fame lies in the number of his squares, streets and avenues. In the eyes of the Comtesse, fame, Rome and the number of His temples were one of the proofs of the existence of God. "Anna," I said to her, "you want to be a statue during your lifetime, a statue with legs to run about everywhere." When she insulted me I answered back, but our quarrels ended by my running away. I would leave the table. The Princesse de Polignac used to remember how she once went to look for me and found me playing checkers with Anne-Jules, the Comtesse's son. One evening—the quarrel arose out of my letter to Jacques Maritain[2]—the Comtesse, in a long nightgown, pursued me, brandishing a chair, out onto the landing. She leaned over, grasping the banisters and cried, "In any case, it's quite simple. If God exists, I should be the first person to be told."

Affectionate quarrels, pretexts for interminable discussions. Most frequently I attacked her for her conventional conception of greatness.

She reproached me for losing dash. Love is not dashing, I replied. Love destroys dash. We say "I love you"; but the moment I select certain people or things when I am ready to die for them, I lose the power of speech and all its range. A virtuoso does not serve music; it serves him. That is why it is preferable to listen to him playing second-rate music. Then he can shine. You shine for lack of love, I told her. Your love is countless and it is nothing. At least you have not committed the crime of manufacturing love, like Barrès. Then the quarrel would start again with redoubled strength. And I would leave. I would go down the rue Cortambert. Opposite the Hôtel Polignac in the avenue Henri-Martin, the asphalt, swollen by the sunshine, absorbed air and formed into a pair of bellows, uttering bird-like cries at night as you walked over it. This detail, and these cries from the pavement, were the last things that woke me and distracted me from my dreams. I went on with the quarrel alone. My heart raged,

[2] Published in 1926, an essay in which Cocteau discusses personal and philosophical problems and writes sadly of friends he has lost. (See p. 104.)

loved and adored—and since time is invented by men, I would find myself instantaneously, without having walked, in the rue d'Anjou, at my own door.

At the window of the cretonne-hung room a box full of hyacinths formed an obstacle that the Comtesse did not surmount. As she always lay stretched out, I believe (unless she breathed in the heliotrope scents of Amphion) that she imagined gardens, flowers and bumble-bees fringed with hair like the eyes of a Persian princess, through this box of hyacinths, those perfumed sentinels that watched, standing stiffly upright, over her light, rare sleep. She slept badly, stuffed herself with sleeping tablets, felt ill and rarely spoke of her sufferings. People believed that she was a malingerer. Marcel Proust was treated as one. To say "I am dead" instead of "I am tired" is imagination. Poets are imaginary invalids. And they die. How surprising! How inconvenient! People think we are made of steel.

Anna saw a thousand doctors. Apart from Madame Lobre, whom she loved and believed, the doctors were excuses for vocal exercises. She did not want her doctors to look after her. She wanted to look after her doctors.

She is dead. Life is dead. She of whom Barrès said, "She is the most sensitive spot in the universe." He spoke too of "her little body that looked like a Spanish Christ." She wanted to be embalmed. I did not dare to see her in that state. I can imagine that, embalmed, she must be like Thaïs in the Musée Guimet. Among a rustling and crackling of old cigars, dry roses and dry bandages, Thaïs floats on her back on the river of the dead. One morning, at the Musée Guimet, I saw a Carmelite priest kneeling by the glass case. He carried the heart and cross of Père de Foucauld. It was Père Charles. He was praying. I had forgotten that the mummy was that of Saint Thaïs.

When I die I shall go to see Anna de Noailles. I shall cross the hallway of clouds. I shall open the door and I shall hear the voice reserved for quarrels: "My dear, you see, there is nothing afterwards, nothing. You remember, I told you so"—and to my eternal delight, everything will start all over again. The Comtesse is talking.

The Empress Eugénie

The time of youthful admiration came to an end, overlapping with the early participation in various artistic fields. From his creative hero worship of actors, Cocteau soon progressed, by way of his early poems, to active work in the theater, and he was lucky enough to be a young man in Paris at the time of Serge Diaghilev's Russian invasion of 1908. Beginning with an exhibition of Russian painters it continued with visits by singers and finally the dancers, who first appeared there in 1909. Cocteau was at once drawn into this magic circle and two years later he began to collaborate in the writing of ballet scenarios.

What counted most for him at this stage was the contact with Diaghilev, whose famous remark "Surprise me" was the most exciting challenge Cocteau ever received. From that moment until his death he was to surprise a great number of people, sometimes even himself. Through Diaghilev he met dancers, painters, composers, forming lifelong relationships with many of them, and these experiences so colored his outlook that the dividing line between the theater and the real world was sometimes almost lost.

His lifelong admiration of theatrical people led him sometimes, unconsciously perhaps, to transform men or women he knew into his own favorite type of stage personality. This explains why he was fascinated by a brief meeting with the Empress Eugénie, who at the end of her life was perhaps not so much a woman as a character from a historical novel. The Second Empire had collapsed in 1870, her husband, formerly Napoleon III, had died in 1873, an exile in England, while her only son had been killed fighting the Zulus in Africa in 1879; but she lived on into a new age, dying in 1920 at the age of ninety-four.

This evocative description, with its moving and comical de-

tails, is more subtle and more impressionistic than many of the others in Portraits-Souvenir, *which were written around Cocteau's early memories. It shows him taking his leave of inspired journalism and gives a hint of how he was to write about people later in life.*

Lucien[1] introduced me to the Empress Eugénie at Cap Martin, where we were living in a hotel with our mothers. The Empress owned the Villa Cyrnos, with its steeply sloping gardens which overlooked the sea, between the property of Madame D, which was infested with croaking frogs, and that of Maria Star. On one side of the wall Maria Star (the pseudonym of Madame S) displayed the chasubles, chains, rings, pendants, croziers and corpulence of a Babylonian bishop; on the other side of the wall lived the most moving and anachronistic woman of the century.

Youth enters and meets age departing. This is an interminable moment, a terrifying minuet through the mists of time. This contact of hands forms a never-ending chain. I had to overcome my shyness and laziness and allow Lucien, a real page-boy in the little court of Cyrnos and Farnborough Hill,[2] to take me to the Empress. It was intensely hot. The crickets hummed like fever and quinine. The sea sparkled and licked itself on the shore.

They say that Tarquinius Superbus lashed at poppies with his whip and cut off their heads—a sign of activity. The Empress detested flowers. She hit them with her stick, pushing them out of her way. We crossed also a dry garden, consisting only of rocks and cactuses. A real Spanish garden with rigid plants, more spiked and bristling than madonnas.

I was beginning to lose countenance, to fear the apparition which would not be long delayed (the Empress was out walking and we were going to meet her), and to imagine Winterhalter's *Decameron*—the Empress, seated in the midst of her maids of honor, infinitely less reassuring than the grenadiers of the guard—when the meeting took place, rapid and unexpected, as dark and small as an accident. And, as with an accident, I had plenty of

[1] Lucien Daudet, grandson of the more famous Alphonse.
[2] The house where the Empress lived in England until her death.

time, as I watched the obstacle come slowly closer, to control my nerves, feel no emotion and not lose my head.

The Empress came out of a winding alley. Madame de Mora and the Comte Clary, who were in attendance, appeared afterwards. Wearing a sort of cassock and a priest-like hat, she climbed up, leaning on a stick like some goat fairy. What struck me first was the small amount of space she occupied, reduced in size like those heads that were shrunk by the savages who killed her son; she was a blot of ink in bright sunshine. And I realized that all that remained of this montgolfier balloon was the charred gasoline tank, the black heart of the poppy. The things that were missing, the things with which one normally associated her were the crinoline, the boating jacket, the spencer, the dangling ribbons, the huge swaying straw hat, the crown of wild flowers and the tiny broken sunshade from Chantilly.

The face was the same. It had kept its delicate oval shape. It looked as though an unhappy young woman had buried her face in her hands too often and that in the end the shape of her fingers had left their imprint upon it. The eyes had kept their heavenly blue but the gaze had been diluted. An expanse of blue water inspected you. This blue, and the black eye-shadow which outlined it, recalled the tattooed eyes of young sailors who are released from prison when they are old. In these old men you find to your surprise the indelible signs of angry beauty.

The Empress stopped: the blue water looked me up and down. Lucien introduced me. "I can no longer decorate poets," she said; "here you are, I can give you this"—and with a rapid movement, she tore off a white bunch of daphne, offered it to me, watched me put it in my buttonhole and went on walking. "Come." I walked beside her. She questioned me about dancing—Isadora Duncan and the *Ballets Russes*. She told me about a firework display the night before at Cap d'Ail. She would stop and sometimes burst out laughing. That voice, and that laughter which broke in two and threw her backwards—where had I heard them before? It was a memory of the bull ring—the laughter and chatter of the young Eugénie de Montijo which were to frighten and fascinate the shy Napoleon III, the laughter and chatter of all

young Spanish women, stamping with their little goat-like feet and fluttering their fans as they applaud the matador making a kill.

"Preceded by her suite." This little joke would hardly have had any meaning at Cyrnos. The Empress exhausted her attendants, trotted along, was surprised that people complained of tiredness and suggested accompanying me part of the way back.

When I took my leave and she invited me to come back again soon, I saw her whole face and her whole frail mourning-clad figure illuminated by a flash of youth, like the lightning-flash of the salamander which brings life into ruins.

I saw the Empress again at the Hôtel Continental, where stupid people reproached her for staying opposite the Tuileries. What could remain from the past to affect a woman who had died several times? Only habit. The habit of living in a certain district, which is stronger than any other.

The Continental preserves the style. The electricity hides beneath the gas globes of the lamp stands. Lucien Daudet led me through the halls with their Boulle furniture and velvet sofas. A brown door with gold markings opened. At the end of a huge drawing-room the Empress was seated, warming herself. The old Comtesse de Pourtalès and the Duc de Montmorency stood by her side; the Duc was wrinkled and cadaverous, covered with moss and lichen, his opera hat under his arm, a marvel of bearing and elegance.

The Empress had heard that women were wearing colored wigs. She questioned me. I replied that this was so, but that I rarely visited the places where one saw them. The Comtesse de Pourtalès was horrified: "Colored wigs! They must be mad." Then the Empress turned around all at once. "My dear," she cried, "we have done other things in our time!" And as the old lady began to contradict her sovereign as far as she could, the Empress, implacable, hoarse and childish, began to rehearse the list of their follies. The crinoline, inspired by Goya's Infantas, the linen panta-lets which showed beneath dresses, tasseled boots, she forgot nothing. And finally, "You, my dear, you had a carriage with glass panels and roses painted on them!" The Comtesse choked: "With roses painted on them!" The Empress was much amused. She was precise. She insisted. The Duc was entirely of her opinion, he unearthed old scandals, old jokes, and old eccentricities. I neither breathed nor moved, trembling lest by some clumsy gesture I should interrupt this astonishing scene, lest I should close the Empress' drawer sharply, make the cock crow and send the ghosts away.

Guillaume Apollinaire

Sadly, Cocteau and Apollinaire were not friends over a long period, for this remarkable poet, half-Italian, half-Polish by birth, died in 1917 only a few years after the two men had met; but the relationship was equal, and Cocteau never refers to Apollinaire as a "master." His influence was deep and lasting. The mysterious sentence L'oiseau chante avec ses doigts, one of the key motifs in the film Orphée, is a line by Apollinaire. The star which so often accompanied Cocteau's signature to his drawings is related to the star-like wound on Apollinaire's forehead, a symbol repeated in the drop of ink that fell from the poet's pen and starred the sheet of paper. Many people, Maurice Sachs among them, have seen Cocteau as a "magician"; Cocteau in his turn acknowledged "magicians" in his life, and Apollinaire was one of the most enduring.

Cocteau wrote about him on various occasions, but this piece, which he wrote for a French literary magazine in 1954, seems to me one of his most expressive tributes. So much about Apollinaire was and still remains indefinable that Cocteau has to write at more length than usual in order to situate him, and makes a particular point of saying that others will analyze him.

Guillaume Apollinaire bewitched us, once and for all. I remember a period when we used to walk through Saint-Germain des Prés, which later took over from Montparnasse. He would say: "We are falling between two stools." It distressed him. He did not know that between these two stools a fall in the opposite direction was imminent which would lead him to become a constellation.

Nobody ever demanded of Apollinaire anything that he could

not or would not give. He was spared the "do this and do that" with which artists are overwhelmed. Nobody reproached him for the books which he wrote with his left hand,[1] as though he were flicking away the ash from a cigarette. People adore in him the poet who marks the page, folds it up and obtains one of those blot tests which have become fashionable.

All these blots are valuable, living, expressive, exquisite in their grace and strength. They limp and blink like stars whose terrible light seems to us subject to the slightest breath of wind.

Their elegance is supreme. It has no connection with the elegance envisaged by frivolity. These blots have an elegance similar to that of animals and trees. What is more, they escape analysis (in which they differ from the tests) and theories like that which attacks Rimbaud, for example. Their secrets are admissible or impenetrable, and, when they are impenetrable, they form objects sufficient unto themselves, whose origin and use escape us, although this is what gives them their air of necessity, the balanced aspect of their organism.

Robert Goffin's book *Rimbaud et Verlaine Vivants* brings real comfort to those who know how much a work suffers when it moves away from its base and wanders about in the minds of others, losing itself at sea.

Tables are only useful for spiritualists now, forming a pretext for the shadowy hands which question them. A man who looks at a table with the eyes of a cabinet-maker and touches it with a cabinet-maker's respect sweeps away the shadowy hands and brings us close to the ciphers beneath which a poet hides in order to live in society, until that same society throws him out of the window or disgusts him and makes him decide to sever his connections with it.

Death has severed connections as far as Apollinaire is concerned. But I suspect that his secrets would have been safe from hatred and that he would have moved among us without any intervention from the police forces which hunt down aristocratic anarchy.

[1] A reference to Apollinaire's work, usually editorial, in connection with erotica, especially the publications of the *Bibliothèque des Curieux*.

France kills its poets. The list of its victims is long. It drives out the unusual. Apollinaire knew this and searched for a label likely to reassure public opinion, which was devoted to schools and placards. He suggested "Orphism." Came Surrealism, which adopted him.

This massacring of poets is no doubt a good thing, indispensable to their efficacity; since the poet is by definition posthumous, he begins to live after his death and during his lifetime he walks with one foot in the grave. This gives him a kind of limp which endows him with an attractive appearance. Apollinaire was not assassinated, however, and the title of one of his books[2] bears witness to the fact. This occurred all the same, through the intermediary of war, which is a social crime, and his nice nature would admit only its grace.

His work never contains the slightest patriotic invective. If he uses the word "boche," he does so with a smile. In his war, sky-blue soldiers move beneath bunches of stars, beneath the delightful fireworks of bombs. In his war he is preoccupied only with his loves and his comrades. At the very moment when his colleagues were kneeling down in front of the guns, he would gather herbs, and when you open one of his books and see the *calligrammes* assuming the graceful outline of lilies of the valley, you are reminded of an herbal.

He gathered herbs between the Seine and the Rhine.

The Seine which flows "propped up by books," the Rhine where the Lorelei sings. He gathers herbs there more sinister than meadow saffron.

Herbalist and alchemist. Even at the front, he concocted strange mixtures and delicious poisons in his mess tin. He sent them to Rouveyre on post cards.

He always used to talk to me about the "event poem," which he placed above all the others.

Zones, Les Colchiques, La Chanson du Mal-aimé, Lettre Océan are "event poems" and, with the possible exception of *Lettre Océan,* had no suspicion of the fact. They reflect a moment of luck when all the dice show double six, when something that

[2] *Le Poète Assassiné,* a collection of prose pieces published in 1916.

could exist and something that gropes blindly in our darkness arrange to meet in broad daylight, on the green table.

One wonders if Hugo, after writing *Booz Endormi* or *Tristesse d'Olympio*, was capable of realizing that he was flying higher than himself, summing himself up and making up for his mistakes.

The "event poem" disconcerts imitators and attracts them. It deceives them, for its solitude remains solitude, even when the flies come on to it. It is incorruptible. No literary fashion removes a scrap of its volume nor of its fires. The poems of which I speak have nothing to do with the poems which are linked with certain actual events, a fact which assures them of momentary prestige and deceives innumerable naïve readers.

The eventfulness of these event poems lies in the fact that they exist. They draw their marvelous quality from no external circumstance. They comment on no event. They are events on which comments are made. They will lend themselves to commentaries in the same way as acts or reigns. As they are born, they cut both the umbilical cord and all the threads which link them to the poet, who is both their father and mother. They follow an orbit which is their own. Those who know how to greet poetry recognize them at first glance.

It can happen that a single line proves this phenomenon and consecrates the poem to which it belongs. This is the event-line.

When Baudelaire writes, "The great-hearted maidservant of whom you were jealous," or "And your feet slumbered in my brotherly hands," the rest of the poem is certainly drawn towards the heights, even if some carelessness works against it.

Poems which represent a total and indivisible event are, I repeat, extremely rare. They can be counted. It is the glory of Apollinaire that he left us several of them.

I shall never tire of describing him. I have shown him in *La Difficulté d'Etre*, heavy and light, sometimes appearing obese and filled with luminous air, like the montgolfier balloons of our childhood days, sometimes struggling against what he himself had released, with the robust fragility of kites as they rear up.

It is hard for me to imagine him without the little leather helmet which protected his wound, a kind of star of the sea whose place had been prophesied by one of Giorgio de Chirico's portraits.[3]

This little helmet seemed to make one with his person and constitute only the device by which he received and transmitted certain codes.

He had round eyes, like the nightingale, and he had the same episcopal gestures and white hands as the specialists whom we saw at cockfights, standing motionless beside a ring spattered with blood and feathers. He was also reminiscent of certain Monte Carlo gamblers, whose anxiety is expressed only through a grave pallor.

When he laughed, with his hand in front of his mouth, like someone yawning, the whole mass of his body shook and became somehow disorganized. And it took a long time for this volcanic disturbance to settle down, after which he assumed again his bishop-like mask.

Bishop, Grand Inquisitor, Duke of Florence, Catherine de Médicis, some being who had become implacable through refinement and splendor.

His knowledge consisted of everything that knowledge neglects, and he unearthed it on the sidelines. He applied himself only to the sidelines. It is there that one finds the principal things: divergences from the direct line, the shameful incidents of history. He retained only anecdotes which had been lost.

These formed his study and his school. And we were his scholars.

In the vast cemetery where we exist, his Saint Elmo fires circulate.

In the vast night where we exist, there glow his lights of Saint John.

Poets console us in fact for the empty words which pile up on earth and let loose catastrophes. They alone know the virtue of simples which can cure everything and which are the deceptive idiom through which nature expresses herself.

The perfect minstrel. That was how Nietzsche defined Schubert. I would define Apollinaire in the same way, as chief

[3] A charcoal drawing, usually assigned to 1916.

of the "lied," between Heine and Rilke. And this can probably be explained by his habit of humming his poems as he wrote them. The song that they translate remains shut in.

The poem sings it. And I am not referring to the musicality of the line, about which everyone is mistaken. I am referring to one language translated into another. I mean a strange language which the poet does not know well and wants to translate into his own, one which would give the poem a false air of clumsiness, an anti-platitude, an exquisite strangeness.

It is almost impossible to describe to the young people of 1953 the little theaters where we applauded *Les Mamelles de Tirésias*[4] and *Couleur du Temps*.[5] We packed into them like the ingredients of a bomb. At this period politics were the politics of literature. Everything for us became explosive, a cause for passion. I have described elsewhere the tribunal which claimed to try Apollinaire after *Les Mamelles*, for he was guilty of doing violence to the Cubistic dogma. And I think I have already described the astonishing spectacle of *Couleur du Temps*.

The legs of wooden figures hanging from clothes hangers represented the aviators. Actresses in mourning formed India ink blots on the *décor* which Vlaminck had cut out of brown paper. A naked woman glinted on it, pink in her cellophane icepack.

This setting, along with Picasso's design for the Bath of the Graces in *Mercure*,[6] remains unforgettable for me. These are the snows of yesteryear.

It is impossible to separate the names of Apollinaire and Picasso. Nobody draws better than Picasso. Nobody wrote better than Apollinaire. Pencil and pen obey them. Strong in their

[4] A surrealist drama in two acts, this is one of Apollinaire's best-known works and probably dates from 1913 or 1914, although Apollinaire stated that he wrote much of it ten years earlier. It was first produced in 1917.

[5] A verse drama, slightly later.

[6] An avant-garde ballet, or "poses plastiques," with music by Erik Satie, choreography by Massine, *décor* and costumes by Picasso. It was produced unsuccessfully in 1924.

mastery, they will be able to twist syntax and bend it to their requirements.

But while Picasso discovers Cubist classicism following Fauvist romanticism and passes from this classicism to a type of lyrical tornado which transports objects, like a thunderbolt, from one significance to another, crushing iron, cutting up shapes, insulting the human face magnificently with affectionate halts and furious fresh starts while he pushes museum exhibits into the streets, while he registers the slightest details of the district where he lives and forces them (posters, signs, children's hopscotch lines or drawings on the wall) to become the signs of his word, while he turns his back on beauty because he runs faster than she does and precedes her,[7] Apollinaire remains the man who loiters along two river banks, the banks of the Seine and the banks of the Rhine. He watches this corrida as a spectator.

If he confided to me one evening his exhaustion with the way in which Cubism and its Aristotelian rules was becoming a form of algebra, architects' plans and the Golden Number, he never tired of Rousseau, Matisse or the violent surprises he demanded from painters, plunging into them like a great bumble-bee into flowers.

Until his death, Picasso represented for him the prince of the movement which displaced lines, murdered boredom, ship-wrecked the weak and proudly upset the traffic.

And yet, in the same preface to the catalogue in which he compared Matisse to an orange cut in two, he compared him to a pearl.

For while Picasso in 1916 caused fewer ravages and did not take his priesthood to the point of sacrilege, Apollinaire examined that gentle and profound light which at the present time directs his poems and fascinates even those who do not understand them.

He died on the day of the Armistice. The viewpoint of our universe is so different from that of others that we thought the town was hung with flags in his honor.

[7] It is interesting to compare this passage with the later portrait of Picasso, pp. 65–78.

My Contemporaries

Picasso and Max Jacob had come in the morning to my apartment in the rue d'Anjou, so that I could telephone to Doctor Capmas. Apollinaire was extremely ill. Excess fat was stifling his heart. It was no doubt this danger which had been indicated by the delightful breathlessness of his speech.

Medicine was powerless. At night we all assembled in the little bedroom in the boulevard Saint-Germain where, gradually, through the magic of a wax taper, the semi-darkness and the silence, his face, emerging alone from the sheets, became unmistakably the decapitated head of Orpheus.

Raymond Radiguet

Raymond Radiguet was only twenty when he died in 1923, yet Cocteau, who was eleven years older, spoke of him as his "examiner." It would be true to say that although Radiguet went through phases of heavy drinking, he had all the same a sobering influence on Cocteau, for his genius expressed itself mainly in plain prose, which cut through the "isms" of the time like a sterilized and withering knife. It has occasionally been alleged that Cocteau wrote Radiguet's novels; this cannot be true, for he would have been incapable of doing so, but it could be suggested that without the presence of Cocteau and his friends the novels might never have been written, or never finished. Ball at Count d'Orgel's *is said to have been dictated to the composer Georges Auric while the group of young men were staying at Le Picquey on the Bassin d'Arcachon during the summer of 1923, a few months before Radiguet's death.*

Cocteau has written about Radiguet on many occasions and has acknowledged the lasting value of his famous anti-ism advice: il faut faire des romans comme tout le monde. *Only a far-sighted man could have seen that a return to classical criteria, at least as far as form was concerned, was infinitely more adventurous at that moment than the so-called avant-garde audacities of the period. Cocteau had been so deeply impressed by Radiguet from every point of view that his own work reflected the influence of the younger man. The two novels* Le Grand Ecart *and* Thomas l'Imposteur, *although not "conventional" in the normal sense, were written in a more straightforward prose than Cocteau had used earlier. He had absorbed Radiguet's lesson and the "examiner" would probably have given him a fairly good mark.*

As far as the personal side of the relationship was concerned,

Radiguet's death left Cocteau heartbroken. He was even referred to as "le veuf sur le toit." He was comforted only by the thought that he had recognized Radiguet's genius to the full during his lifetime. The text which follows is that of a radio talk given to commemorate the twenty-year anniversary of the novelist's death. A few years later Ball at Count d'Orgel's was read as a radio serial.

In one of his poems Rilke writes: "Beauty is the starting point of terror." This sentence sums up the ground covered by Raymond Radiguet between the moment of his appearance and his death.

He appeared to us at the age of fourteen and amazed us with his poems, his sovereign intelligence, his calmness and silent wisdom. He died at the age of twenty of typhoid fever, in the nursing home in the rue Piccini, leaving France with two masterpieces: *The Devil in the Flesh* and *Ball at Count d'Orgel's.*

Nobody can appreciate to the full this miraculous meteor, which was comparable in the history of the novel to the appearance of Rimbaud in poetry, without knowing the state of literature at the time.

On one side there was the dreariest kind of conventionality and on the other a remarkable chaos made up of all kinds of experimental work. These daring experiments, like tongues of fire, or alcohol-burning flames which spurted through the smallest cracks and devoured everything (and each other at the same time), were Radiguet's classics. He learned to read among extremes. And his short-sighted eye contemplated in a meditative fashion the most astonishing enterprise, which consisted of contradicting the immediate, placing revolutionary force in the service of darkness, revealing night as it were in broad daylight.

And not only did this boy teach us elegance, that is the concealment of thunderbolts, but he also influenced us and dictated to us deep-lying motives which affected us profoundly.

Raymond Radiguet lived in Montparnasse and Montmartre, the two mountains where invention continually rises to the surface. He grew up among painters, poets and journalists. He drank a great deal and withdrew into almost total silence.

One day when we were wandering from studio to studio with

Picasso, Modigliani, Kisling, Max Jacob, we went to see the painter H. who was completing a "still life." He showed it to us and when we said nothing he muttered "It's not finished. . . ." Radiguet, to my amazement, opened his mouth. Staring vaguely at the still life, pressing the single lens of his perpetually broken spectacles into his eye, he said to the painter H.: "It would be human to finish it off."

I think this is the only time Radiguet uttered a witticism one can quote, for the possessor of this proud mind detested clever remarks and only spoke in order to explain the work of our group.

Our group . . . what am I saying? There were innumerable groups and they fought among themselves. There was Cubism and Dadaism, and isms grew like weeds. Radiguet enjoyed the impunity of his extreme youth and his genius. People liked him, flattered him, took him everywhere. He lived with his family at the Parc Saint-Maur. If he missed his train he would hop along in the dark, thin, blind and tousled, his pockets full of scraps of crumpled paper from which he read us his poems. He would go back, either to Montmartre or Montparnasse, and sleep in someone's studio, anywhere, among the canvases, tubes of paint and easels. The creation of *The Devil in the Flesh* was all the more surprising because Radiguet was torn between the certainty of writing something marvelous and the moodiness of a lazy schoolboy.

At Le Picquey, by the Bassin d'Arcachon, he had to be locked in before he would work, he used to escape through the window, and if he had promised to write he would scribble something, just anything, in illegible handwriting.

Afterwards he would behave like a Chinese sage, rolling cigarettes, bending over exercise books until his face touched them and giving the impression that he was a good scholar, a grave and conscientious writer. The outcome of these alternating moods and the long gaps during which he lived in terrifying chaos was a masterpiece of French literature: *The Devil in the Flesh*.

The scandal, which was a mixture of admiration and anger, was due to the amount of publicity, unknown at that time, which Grasset gave to the book; the author insisted on it, asserting that "works should come into the hands of those who cannot read."

37

In fact Radiguet had published a book worthy of *Adolphe*; its novelty was all the more extraordinary because it caused astonishment through its extremely simple style, one which was no longer fashionable, and nobody expected it. In addition to this novelty Radiguet was a prodigy. It was unheard of: a boy of fifteen writing about the behavior of people of his own age and not leaving it to those who could do no more than remember it. He turned a searchlight onto the darkness of childhood and revealed it to us with harsh clarity.

The Devil in the Flesh opened the doors to the young. Before this, young people had been despised, doors had been shut in their faces. Afterwards publishers combed Paris and the provinces in search of a new miracle.

But miracles are rare. Like Rimbaud, Radiguet remained the only one of his kind. It is twenty years since he died at the age of twenty, and he became the novelist of youth. His shadow, which dominates young people, is only twenty years old and his work has not aged. When he died, consumed by the fire which devoured him calmly, he left us another masterpiece, *Ball at Count d'Orgel's*.[1] We corrected the proofs religiously and published the book, which was at last praised by all those who had reproached him over *The Devil in the Flesh*, holding it against him as a fantastic piece of impertinence.

On December 12, 1943, nothing remains of this excitement, a mere news item of the past. There survive only, in the literary heavens, the two books which, together with *Les Joues en Feu*,[2] form a burning constellation, not far from the stars of Benjamin Constant and Madame de La Fayette.[3]

---

[1] This second novel was published in 1920, shortly after Radiguet's death, with a preface by Cocteau.

[2] A collection of poems.

[3] The author of the 17th-century masterpiece *La Princesse de Clèves*. Cocteau wrote an admiring preface for the Nonesuch Press edition in English, published in London in 1943.

Marcel Proust

Although he discovered "masters" for himself until late in life, it was soon after his first contacts with the world of the Ballets Russes *that some of Cocteau's more equal two-way friendships seemed to mature and acquire depth. Marcel Proust was twenty-one years older, and no two men could have written in more widely contrasting styles, but they had a good deal in common, especially their social background and their preoccupation with masculine relationships. Perhaps Cocteau did not recognize himself at the time as "Octave" in the great work, but he genuinely admired it and reviewed Proust's writing with the penetrating enthusiasm that only he could achieve.*

It is interesting to compare the description of Proust which follows with the much later portrait in La Difficulté d'Etre, *where some of the allusions are repeated, notably the references to Jules Verne and the bearded Sadi Carnot. My own preference is, however, for this passage from* Opium, *for the book was written in the late twenties, not many years after Proust's death, and I find the note more personal, more intense and dramatic.*

It is impossible for me to remember any first meeting with Proust. Our group has always treated him as a famous man. I see him, with a beard, seated on the red cushions at Larue's[1] (1912). I see him, without a beard, at Madame Alphonse Daudet's,[2] with Jammes[3] plaguing him like a gadfly. I find him again, dead, with the beard he had at the start. I see him, with and without a beard,

[1] The famous and fashionable restaurant.

[2] Widow of the author of *Lettres de Mon Moulin.*

[3] Francis Jammes (1868–1938), best known for his novels and poems about animals and country life.

in that room of cork, dust and phials, either in bed, wearing gloves, or standing in a sordid washroom, buttoning a velvet waistcoat over a poor square torso which seemed to contain his mechanism, and eating noodles standing up.

I see him among the dust-sheets. They lay over the chandelier and the armchairs. Naphthalene lit up the shadows. He stood erect against the chimney-piece in the drawing-room of this *Nautilus* like a character out of Jules Verne, or else, near a picture hung with crape, wearing a dress coat, like Carnot dead.

Once, announced by Céleste's voice over the telephone, he came to get me at three in the afternoon so that I could go with him to the Louvre to see Mantegna's *Martyrdom of Saint Sebastian*.[4] This canvas then occupied a place in the same room as *Madame Rivière*, *Olympia* and *Le Bain Turc*. Proust was like a lamp lit in broad daylight, the ringing of a telephone in an empty house.

Another time he was supposed to come (perhaps) at about eleven o'clock at night. I was with my neighbor on the first floor, she of whom he wrote to me: "When I was twenty she refused to love me; now that I am forty and have been the delight of the Duchesse de G——, must she refuse to read me?"

I had asked to be told when he came. At midnight I went back upstairs. I found him on my landing. He was waiting for me, sitting on a seat in the darkness. "Marcel," I cried, "why didn't you go in at least and wait for me? You know the door is left ajar." "Dear Jean," he replied, in the voice that he used to muffle with his hand, the voice that was a moan, a laugh, "dear Jean, Napoleon had a man shot because he had waited for him in his room. Of course I would only have read Larousse, but there could have been letters and so on lying about."

Alas, someone has stolen the book in which he wrote verses for me. I remember:

"Covering me with watered silk and sable,
Letting no ink from his big black eyes overflow,

[4] In 1911 Ida Rubinstein appeared in Gabriele d'Annunzio's drama *Le Martyre de Saint Sébastien*, with music by Debussy.

Like a sylph on the ceiling, a ski on the snow,
Next to Nijinsky Jean leapt on the table."

We were having supper after the theater with the Russian ballet.

"It was in the crimson salon of Larue
Where the gold, of doubtful taste, was never rusty,
A doctor's beard, in thick and florid manner
Repeated: My presence may be incongruous to you
But if only one man remains I shall be he,
And my heart succumbed to the beats of *Indiana*."

Was this doctor, who knew the exact terms, used in the composition of Cottard? *Indiana* was the tune of the moment.

At this period we used to send each other poetic addresses. The Post Office did not get annoyed. For instance:

Postman, bear these words, till they take their leave of you
At Boulevard Haussmann, Marcel Proust's, 102.
102, Boulevard Haussmann, all speed unloosed,
Run, postman, to Marcel Proust!

Proust replied with envelopes covered with a spidery scrawl. In alexandrines he described the rue d'Anjou from the boulevard Haussmann to the Faubourg Saint-Honoré.

Near to the cave where Froment-Meurice flew one day,
Near to the ineffable Nadar. . . .

I have forgotten the beginning and I am cutting out the end because flattery linked with reproaches was his method of friendship.

I ask myself through what feats of love my dear friends Antoine Bibesco, Lucien Daudet and Reynaldo Hahn kept their balance. In spite of numerous letters (there was one very fine one about the revival of *Parade*;[5] he compared the acrobats to the Dioscuri and called the horse "great swan with wild movements")

---

[5] Cocteau's *ballet réaliste*, first produced in 1917, with the collaboration of Picasso and Erik Satie.

we stopped seeing each other as the result of a ridiculous scene. I had gone to the boulevard Haussmann as a neighbor, without hat and coat. When I came in I said "I've no coat, I'm frozen."

He wanted to give me an emerald, which I refused. Two days later I had a cold. A tailor came to take my measurements for a fur-lined coat. The emerald was presumably intended in the first place to facilitate the purchase. I sent the tailor away and Marcel Proust bore me a grudge on this account. To his epistle of grievances he added others, going on for twelve pages, which he charged me to pass on to the Comte de B——. This interminable indictment ended with a postscript: *In fact, say nothing.*

I have recounted elsewhere (*Hommage à Marcel Proust, N.R.F.*) the anecdote about the tip to the concierge at the Ritz Hotel. "Can you lend me fifty francs?" "Here you are, Monsieur Proust." "Keep it, it's for you."

Needless to say, the concierge was to receive three times the amount next morning.

It is agreed that Marcel Proust did not write *romans à clef*, but certain of his friends provided many ingredients in his mixtures. He could not understand therefore why the model, whose faults he depicted as charm, would refuse to read his book, not out of rancor, for the model was incapable of recognizing himself, but out of weak-mindedness. He (Proust) would then demand, with outbursts of childish anger, something analogous to Fabre's huge success with insects.

In order to understand the atmosphere at Proust's, go to the Comédie Française. Push open the last door on the right down a little corridor leading from the stage to the big green room. It used to be Rachel's dressing-room. There, in an atmosphere as hot as a furnace, you will see dust-sheets, a harp, a painter's easel, a harmonium, glass covers for clocks, bronzes, ebony pedestals, empty glass cases, illustrious dust . . . in short, you will be at Proust's waiting for Céleste to let you in.

I note this resemblance because of Rachel and La Berma, because of everything that coincidence arouses in us by way of sacred riddles.

Maurice Sachs

One of the most refreshing, if old-fashioned aspects of Cocteau's writing is his lack of destructiveness. When he wrote that he loved loving and hated hate he meant it; since he was no saint he obviously felt resentment from time to time, and the expression of these feelings would find their way into conversations or letters, but rarely into the semi-permanent status of books. He was capable of hero worship to an extent that many people would find naïve; if there was anything he disliked in a person or a work he would literally forget about it. He did not pretend that it was not there; for him it simply did not exist. In the portraits quoted earlier in this book Cocteau did not exhort his readers either to admire or devalue Edouard de Max or Catulle Mendès. He merely wanted everyone else to love them as he did. Their absurdities are exploded with gentle laughter, and the author, plus his readers, laughs with them rather than at them. This is perhaps not such a difficult feat, for these loving portraits were drawn from a distance; there is rarely a feeling of adult involvement.

Even an enfant terrible eventually grows up, and later in life Cocteau became involved with various complex people, caught up in relationships full of contradictions, unexplained factors and, no doubt, suffering. Cocteau's version in each case is not the full story; the literary historian will have to read the other side, as Cocteau's friends or ex-friends wrote it, and also the assessments of disinterested parties, if any such can be said to exist. Two of the strangest and most intriguing cases are those of Maurice Sachs and André Gide.

In 1932 Maurice Sachs, who did not claim to be a writer, lived by his wits and wrote extremely well, published La Décade de l'Illusion in which he put down his impressions of Paris and its

*personalities in the 1920's, about which he had previously lectured
in the United States. The book was dedicated to Jean Cocteau,
"to whom I owe the most exquisite years of my youth, in token
of a deep, respectful and fraternal affection."*

There is a whole section entitled The Magicians, *in which the
first chapter is about Cocteau, followed by pieces about Maritain,
Max Jacob and Picasso. Sachs describes with admiration, but not
without lucidity, his early memories of Cocteau and all that
surrounded him: his charming intelligent mother, the valet Cyprien,
the cook who wrote what might have been* romans-fleuve, *but
nobody knew, the antediluvian lift, the lamps; Cocteau himself,
wearing black pajamas in a room full of artistic clutter. His young
admirer goes on to describe Cocteau's peculiar brilliance and rapid
intelligence, his understanding of the young, his wish to be the
first to mention a name. There is no criticism, but it is clear that
Sachs understood the mechanism of Cocteau's personality as well
as anybody has ever done. It is a lyrical tribute, but it is not
fulsome; nobody has ever found it easy to write about magic, for
the rational-minded do not often admit its existence and those
who are probably most sensitive to it cannot always express what
they feel.*

*In any case, it is important for anyone interested in the
Cocteau-Sachs situation to have read this piece first, for as far as I
know it is the earliest written version of the relationship.*

Then in 1946 appeared Le Sabbat, *which Sachs had begun before the war and apparently sold the idea to a publisher in 1939.
In the meantime he had died in Germany, died miserably, horribly.*
Le Sabbat, *which was later translated into English twice in twelve
years, is a well-written* confession d'un enfant du siècle, *combining
a personal story with much about the literature and art of the
period. The personal side is mainly concerned with homosexual
relationships of various kinds and an attempt, which failed, to
become a Catholic. In her autobiographical* récit La Bâtarde[1]
Violette Leduc describes her reactions when she read Le Sabbat
in manuscript: she was living with Sachs at the time, during the

[1] The English translation by Derek Coltman was published by Farrar,
Straus & Giroux in 1965.

German occupation of France. She told him that the book was good but that the pages about Cocteau were horrible and she felt they should be modified or cut out. As though ashamed of his early admiration, Sachs had attacked Cocteau on every front: he found him to be unoriginal in every way, a dangerous influence on the young, a mere animateur, *hated by all the writers and painters whom he claimed to be his friends, and, worst of all, a man with no heart, incapable of feeling. Who will ever know all that had happened between or around the two men? Does it matter? Can we forget incisive remarks which may contain a grain of truth? Since Sachs wrote well and most people find destructiveness entertaining, it is unfortunately this portrait of Cocteau which has remained in many people's minds and has acquired a semi-permanent, almost unchallenged status.*

In 1952 Cocteau published Le Journal d'un Inconnu, *an inward-looking, rather sad book about himself and his own quest for personality and values. This is what he wrote about the author of* La Décade de l'Illusion *and* Le Sabbat.

Maurice Sachs had extreme charm. This charm asserts itself after his death. I could not say either where or how I met him. He hardly ever left my house. He haunted the nursing homes where my health forced me to stay for long periods. His kindly, completely open face was so familiar to me that I cannot remember a time when I did not know him. If he stole from me, he did it in order to buy me presents. And if I mention thefts, it is because he boasted about them.

When Maurice was broke he used to stuff his pockets with toilet paper. He would make it rustle and believed his pockets were full of banknotes. That gives me confidence, he used to say.

I couldn't complain that I was taken in. It was nobody's fault but mine. I have always found thieves more likable than policemen. Not everyone can succeed in being robbed. And you must have confidence. I had it with Sachs. I repeat that he gave me more than he took and took in order to give. This kind of theft cannot be confused with sordid theft, or with theft which displays a kind of inventive genius against which no similar genius can protect us.

One year when I was staying at Villefranche, Maurice took away in a handcart the entire contents of my room in Paris. My books, drawings, correspondence and manuscripts. He sold them in bundles, without going through them. He imitated my handwriting so well that everyone was taken in. I was still living in the rue d'Anjou. He went to see my mother with a forged letter in which I gave him a free hand.

While he was editing a series of books for Gallimard, volumes by Apollinaire and Proust, in which they had written me letters on the flyleaves, were circulating in the sale-rooms. They were on show in shop windows. Since I was made responsible for this scandal I had to explain things to Gallimard. He ordered Sachs to come and see him, telling him that he could not let him keep his job. Sachs asked to be given a few moments. He disappeared and came back with a letter from me which had just been written. The letter requested him to sell at once my books, correspondence and manuscripts. "You see," said Maurice, "how far I can forgive Jean for his fantastic ideas. I'll burn his letter." He set fire to it with his lighter. When Gaston Gallimard described this conjuring trick to me he said that it was the burning of the letter which finally convinced him. And we laughed at Maurice's skill: he had proved his innocence by destroying a forgery.

Even when he was unmasked Maurice continued to take in those he had deceived. He assumed that people laugh at the misadventures of others without fearing for one second that the same things might happen to them. During the Occupation the Jews entrusted him with sables and jewelry. And if I am asked what was my attitude when I was staying on the Côte d'Azur and the bookshops told me they had suspect goods in their possession, I shall reply that I was suffering from *la cagne*. *La cagne* is a Toulon malady. In the past the Préfet Maritime's car would drive around any *cagnard* who was lying asleep in the roadway. *Cagne* is laziness, the Italian *far niente*. Maurice had *la cagne* too. His laziness made him money. It made him fatter and he let himself sink right down into it.

Shortly before he left for Germany he telephoned me one morning, after a year's silence. He was going to die in the Hôtel de Castille. He begged me to come.

In his room at the Hôtel de Castille I found him in bed and very pale. "You were the only one I loved," he said. "Your friendship stifled me. I wanted to deprive myself of it. I wrote lies and insults about you. Forgive me. I've ordered them to be destroyed." Maurice did not die in the Hôtel de Castille. He met death in Hamburg, in terrible circumstances. His books were not destroyed. On the contrary, they are being published, some through our common friend Yvon Belaval. Others, owned by Gérard Mille, are waiting.

I do not share the opinion of my friends who are angered by these insults. Maurice told me the truth, his version of it, as we all do. I believe that the insults he directed at me show that a deep impression had been made upon him. This at least is the angle from which I observe them. He used to create any type of weapons for himself and assail me with them, without rhyme or reason. You could guess that he didn't mean a word of what he said. Anyone who doesn't understand why he attacked both himself and me is incapable of understanding what he wrote. He drew his fluid from this intense urge to drive out the poison that caused him to swell up. His method is defensive and offensive. His dash towards death, which could be taken for flight, was the proof of this.

Maurice Sachs is a typical example of self-defense against the invader. The more he offends the harder he strikes himself. And he also beats his breast in accordance with the ritual of his fellow-believers at the wall of Jerusalem. This preoccupation with self-inflicted blows is the reason why he fascinates people and enjoys posthumous success. But his cynicism would interest nobody if it consisted only of confessions and lies. It is interesting because of its passionate nature. Maurice had a passion for others and for his own personality. His writings are the battleground for the fight he conducted between these two feelings. His youth prevented him from making them cohabit. If he wanted to live, he had to kill. But he only aimed at the visible person. The other escaped him.

Long were the roads which led him to this method. He gave himself over to friendship frankly and without calculation. Neither

Max Jacob nor I had any cause to complain of his friendship. He respected us. He never said *tu* to me. I said *tu* to him and as a rule youth does not experience this shade of meaning. I was often embarrassed by the fact that very young poets used to say *tu* to Max Jacob.

After writing *Le Potomak*[2] I decided to construct a morality for myself. But it was far from being constructed when I went over to the attack. Maurice's morality did not exist. With great skill he suddenly decided to make himself a negative one. A morality with an absence of morals. From that moment he worked at it with all his active laziness. None of us suspected that he was writing all the time. Nobody ever saw him writing. It is true that he began to write when my friends' attitudes ordered me to stop seeing him.

Maurice wrote without a break. He told his own story. He dared to acquire relief by the display of what people call baseness and which is no more than obedience to instincts which are condemned by current morality. As far as his confessions about sexual life are concerned, nature mixes up morals in her machine. Films of the vegetable kingdom, which I have mentioned earlier, tell us about this. Nature alternates her economy and prodigality through a risky use of sex. For if her creatures used the pleasure accompanying the reproductive act for this purpose only, she would fill her living space. She tends towards visual disorder in order to protect her invisible order. The wise disorder could be found in the Pacific islands; the young natives behaved in the normal way and the women gave birth to their babies in cow dung so that only the strongest would survive—until Europeans came to bring order, that is, to bring dresses, alcohol, preaching, over-population and death.

Sachs does not look so far. He slides down his slope. This slope will perhaps supply an instructive document to the court whose sentence is feared by so many young men who believe themselves guilty. I know that he shows off and deceives people. But on the whole, reading between the lines, I approve of the

[2] (1913–1914). Listed in *Poésie du Roman*. First published in 1919.

fact that he opposes hypocrites and persists in defending what is false in order that people can sense what is true.

If I try to remember Maurice, I don't look for him in books. I look at the fascinating years when literary politics divided our milieux, bringing them closer or farther apart. Maurice used to run backwards and forwards between one camp and the other. He was not a traitor. He listened, laughed, helped and put himself out in order to be useful. I scolded him pretty often.

When he entered the seminary I warned Maritain.[3] I knew that he was doing it to avoid paying his debts. Maritain took no notice. In his nobility he put his hopes in this refuge. He would save Maurice from debts more serious and take them upon himself. Maurice became a seminarist. We saw him wearing a cassock and bringing American cigarettes and a bathtub into his cell. His delightful grandmother, Madame Strauss, was in despair because you couldn't wash there.

One day, at Juan-les-Pins, I advised him, since he was behaving very badly, to return to civilian life. He was already bored with playing a part. He gave way gracefully and his charm was such that the Reverend Father Pressoir, the seminary Provincial, reproached me for having been "so quick on the job."

Poor Maurice. If he had not formed the avant-garde for a period when commandos of all types were in fashion, what would be known about him? I approve of him for having given an air of strength to his weaknesses. Whether I like it or not, my morality demands that I forgive him, and welcome him into my Panthéon.

[3] Jacques Maritain, b. 1882, the outstanding Catholic thinker. See also Cocteau's *Lettre à Jacques Maritain* and Sachs's *Le Sabbat.*

André Gide

*Cocteau's long relationship with André Gide shows various strange
parallels with the situations vis-à-vis Maurice Sachs. The basic
difference lies of course in the fact that Gide was a great writer
(whether we find him a likable man is another matter) while
Maurice Sachs, who wrote well, was a moral reprobate. Perhaps
the most detailed version of the Cocteau-Gide relationship, personal but not intimate, was that described in the conversation with
Colin-Simard published in the* Poésie Critique.[1] *There is also an
interesting passage in* Journal d'un Inconnu, *but a good brief
evocation of the relationship, one which is less well known, is this
article from the* Nouvelle Revue Française, *written in 1951 shortly
after Gide's death.*

One cannot assess André Gide as a straight line; he wavered,
and yet his line was meant to be straight. For the flexibility of this
sort of line appears not in geometrical fashion but through the
strange geometry and remarkable perspectives of the human soul.

Arthur Cravan, who was the original Lafcadio,[2] tells us that
after Gide's visit to the *quais* by the Seine, he watched him
through the window. Gide, he wrote, could have chosen between
the windows of a wonderful shop selling shells and those of a
second-hand bookshop. He hesitated, then decided on the bookshop.

This note by Lafcadio shows us Gide perpetually torn between life and the books which praise it. Whenever he traveled
Gide used to catch and classify insects, make collections of plants,

[1] The original publication was in *Le Livre Contemporain*, Amiot-
Dumont, Paris, 1952.

[2] In *Les Caves du Vatican*, 1914, described as a *sotie*.

or go for a swim between reading two acts of a Shakespeare play or two chapters from Goethe.

These endless ups and downs, which he summed up in the phrase, "Extremes touch me," make his work fascinating. A man's voice tells me a great deal. When Proust died it was his voice that I analyzed in the *NRF*.[3] Gide's used to go up and down, becoming sometimes thinner, sometimes fuller; it was musical and tortuous. He knew how to use it for emphasizing some term to which, like a painter, he would add a touch of white light, like the dot for which Chinese portrait-painters charge so much when they add it, during the last sitting, to the model's eye.

Sometimes it sounded as though he was hauling words up from the depths of a tank.

My relationships with Gide were malicious and forgiving. He teased me and loved me, as can be seen from the personal letters he wrote me alongside the journal in which he often revealed himself highly unfair towards me.

One had to understand him and not feel stupidly hurt by the sallies of a deeply susceptible nature which resembled that of Rousseau, which may seem surprising in a descendant of the Encyclopédistes. This mixture constitutes the entire beauty of a man who turned against himself as often as he turned against others. He judged both others and himself with one and the same pen and was never afraid of contradicting himself, since he was not bound by any commitment outside himself.

This constant exchange between an old teacher and a young pupil, between the clever boy and the brilliant duffer, produced a distillation which defied analysis, unless the heart enters into it.

It is a long time since we crossed swords and last year, during long stays at my house at Milly, we spoke of these incidents like old family quarrels. He wanted me to make a film of *Isabelle*.[4] I advised him to aim higher and try a shortened version of *Les Caves du Vatican*.

There was nothing more youthful and lighthearted than the production of *Les Caves* at the Comédie Française. It gave us the

[3] Reproduced in *Poésie Critique*, Paris, 1959.
[4] Published in 1911, a *récit* about the discovery of a family secret.

same delight we had found when children, in the fairy-tale shows at the Châtelet and the presentation of *Round the World in Eighty Days* which were our first revelation of the theater.

There was never any sign of pedantry or false earnestness. Never any sign of a message, although Lafcadio gave rise to imitations and his disciples resembled the Illuminists, who wanted to carry the methods of Luther to extremes.

Gide once showed me the delightful cemeteries of Varengeville and Cuverville, and while we were there he talked to me about death without any fear. Before I left for Egypt he told me that he was amused by the way his attacks of illness had pulled his mouth out of shape. He surprised me by this bravado in the face of physical suffering.

He took the contradictions within his own character to great lengths, mixing caution, fear, extreme rashness and unawareness of danger, as children do.

A cheerful, child-like brightness shone through the ashes and embers of his late years. You could see it in his gaze, this gaze which penetrated everything in spite of the lassitude of age.

The last vision I have of Gide is that of an Erasmus-like figure in a black skullcap, wearing a dressing-gown, surrounded with books and pensive objects, by a piano at which he used to relax by letting Chopin express himself in his place.

No one can prove better than Gide that every serious work is a self-portrait and that the resemblance to the painter is more important than the resemblance to the model, whom the painter only uses as a pretext.

Jean Paulhan wrote to me saying "The moment Gide died he became petrified, he turned completely into stone."

I recognize in this the privilege of kings whom death turns into recumbent statues, and who move over the deep waters.

As Cocteau himself mentions, the entries in Gide's Journal, the so-called private writing which was obviously intended for the public, are complementary reading here. As far back as August, 1914, Gide recorded Cocteau's reaction to the war and his own reaction to an apparently frivolous young man: "I had no pleasure in seeing him again, despite his extreme kindness; but he is incapable of serious-

ness and all his thought, his witticisms, his sensations, all the extraordinary brilliance of his customary conversation shocked me like a luxury article displayed in a period of famine and mourning. . . . *When speaking of the slaughter of Mulhouse he uses amusing adjectives and mimicry; he imitates the bugle call and the whistling of the shrapnel. Then, changing subjects since he sees that he is not amusing me, he claims to be sad; he wants to be sad with the same kind of sadness as you, and suddenly he adopts your mood and explains it to you.* . . . *The odd thing is that I think he would make a good soldier. He asserts that he would and that he would be brave too. He has the carefree attitude of the street urchin; it is in his company that I feel most awkward, the most heavy, the most gloomy."*

Cocteau's behavior in public was like a descant to his psychological demeanor: through contrast and counterpoint the two enhanced each other. This was the apparently unfeeling man who later wrote Thomas l'Imposteur,[5] first published in 1923. There are other references in Gide's Journal which record his failure to enjoy Parade, Antigone, Le Grand Ecart. It would in fact have been very strange if Gide had liked them; and it was a touching idea of Cocteau's to dedicate Mon Premier Voyage,[6] his own version of Round the World in Eighty Days, to the dour, unhappy Gide. It could hardly have compensated for the fact that according to Maurice Sachs many young men had taken down the photographs of Gide from their walls and replaced them with pictures of Cocteau.

[5] The English translation by Dorothy Williams was published by The Noonday Press in 1957 as *The Impostor*, reprinted 1966 by Citadel Press.

[6] Published as *My Journey Round the World*, by Peter Owen Ltd., 1958, in a translation by W. J. Strachan. The French edition was published in 1937.

Amedeo Modigliani

After these tangled relationships and the suffering that they caused it comes as a relief to read a portrait-essay which is written from a cool distance; this description of Modigliani was composed in 1950, long after the painter's tragic death, but it is very much more than an admiring tribute or an enthusiastic portrait-souvenir. *Cocteau remarks that when Modigliani was painting his portrait they became "close friends." But was anyone ever a "close friend" of Modigliani? Some people came close to him, but I am not sure if "friendship" as most people understand it was a feeling in which the young self-exiled Italian could ever have participated.*

Yet in the background even of this quasi-dispassionate portrait some question marks remain. Was this part of the "public relations" work which, according to Maurice Sachs, was the only reason why Picasso and other painters tolerated Cocteau? And would it be fair to say that in writing this piece Cocteau seems bent on reminding the reader that Modigliani painted his portrait? In any case, I have left the first section intact, for as his lead-in Cocteau has made a rough outline sketch of Montparnasse, its atmosphere and its landscape.

It is one of the wonderful things about Paris that from time to time the whole essence of the city seems to become concentrated in one quarter, the haunt of painters, poets and art-lovers. In bygone days, it was Montmartre, and Montparnasse; nowadays, it is Saint-Germain-des-Prés which exercises this strange attractive power.

In 1916, during the war, it was still Montparnasse. I was introduced to the artistic milieu by Picasso, whose windows overlooked the Montparnasse cemetery. He wanted to paint me in Harlequin's costume, and after the sittings we used to visit the Cubist studios. We always finished up at the Café de la Rotonde.

The Rotonde, the Dôme and a restaurant on the corner of the boulevards Raspail and Montparnasse enclose what then looked like a square in a provincial town, a favorite pitch for coster-mongers, with grass growing between the cobblestones. This was our promenade, our haven and our kingdom. I succeeded in getting myself adopted by the natives—a necessary first step for a visitor from the other Bank, though the inhabitants of the Montmartre of Max Jacob, Reverdy and Juan Gris arrived without passport formalities by the North-South Underground.

On rare occasions, we ventured beyond the tacitly accepted boundaries; we crossed the Seine and wandered in our rope-soled slippers from Paul Guillaume's shop to the windows of the Bern-heims, and from there to Paul Rosenberg's. Later Léonce Rosen-berg's became a regular meeting-place, thanks to the sessions de-voted to "the modern poets," held among Cubist canvases and all sorts of artistic objects belonging to the reign of Napoleon III.

In Montparnasse I continued to wear my Right Bank costume, or my uniform (which I am wearing in Picasso's drawing); in 1916, I was serving in Belgium and put in an appearance only when I was on leave. I mention this, because the attire affected by the Montparnassians was destined to become legendary, although, in reality, it was not a question of negligence, nor of a deliberate flouting of conventionality. The Montparnassians used up in Paris the overalls, pullovers, shirts and sandals left over from seaside holidays. The cowboys and Indians came later; and, finally, fashion established itself here too and disguises became the order of the day.

Modigliani was handsome. Handsome, grave and romantic. He worked at Kisling's studio, in the rue Joseph-Bara, not far from the building in which Salmon used to smoke his ancient pipe, surrounded by walls of books.

If I close my eyes, I can still see our square, with Modigliani stamping out a sort of bear-like dance, while Kisling repeats in-cessantly, "Come on, come on home." He refuses by a gesture of his black, curly head. We try to persuade him, and Kisling resorts to force. He grabs hold of the red sash and pulls. Modigliani changes the movement, raising his hands as in Spanish dances; he snaps his fingers and turns round and round. The red sash unwinds, interminably; Kisling goes—Modigliani bursts into a terrible laughter, and goes on stamping more heartily than ever.

If I open my eyes, I can still see our old square—full of hurrying pedestrians, cars, omnibuses and coaches bringing sight-seers to visit the ruins haunted by our ghosts. All the rest is no more; and Rodin's statue of Balzac now stands, motionless, where Modigliani, in the same stance, and himself like a bronze statue, resisted our efforts to take him home. . . .

Amedeo Modigliani was born in 1884, in Leghorn, of a Jewish family. His mother, the widow of a ruined banker, divined his talent, and made him study in the studios of Florence and Venice. In 1906, she sent him to Paris.

Refined by illness (he was tubercular), he had the air of a true aristocrat. Alcohol, drugs, overwork and poverty gave him an outlook on life in which tenderness and cynicism were mingled.

He lived for six years in Montmartre, wandering from café to café, from one hovel to another, sour-tempered, generous and loyal. In 1913, he descended from the Butte and settled (sic!) in Montparnasse, floating uncertainly about, with no fixed abode, and searching on his nightly peregrinations for a world already dead, or not yet born.

He met the English poetess Beatrice Hastings, who sustained him for a while; but from the early days in Kisling's studio to the final period at Zborowski's, his drawings and nudes remained unsold.

Zborowski was poor, but he sacrificed everything to help Modigliani. He gave him an exhibition—which caused a scandal; the police had to intervene.

His marriage, and the child born of it, did not bring Modigliani the hoped-for calm. At the age of thirty-six, he died in the hospital in a raging fever, murmuring, "Cara, cara Italia." On the day of his funeral, his wife committed suicide by jumping from a fifth-floor window.

But we never asked him about his origins; he belonged to

Montparnasse, he frequented the haunt of the intelligent and animated it with his magnificent, drunken presence—that was enough for us.

While he was painting my portrait in oils, we became close friends. I had a sitting every day at three o'clock in Kisling's studio. I was sitting for both painters, and in Kisling's portrait Picasso may be seen in the background, in a check shirt, drawing on a table. Modigliani's portrait (his prices were between five and fifteen francs) has traveled widely, and enjoyed an immense success; but we were not then concerned with the results of our actions; none of us saw things from the historical viewpoint—we merely tried to live, and to live together. As a result, the story of Modigliani is undocumented, with the exception of a few photographs which I took one morning in the Rotonde—and his works. But they are sufficient.

Modigliani was our aristocrat. His drawing is supremely elegant; his line is often so attenuated as to be the mere ghost of a line, but it is never blurred. He does not stretch the outline of a face, or emphasize its lack of symmetry, by blinding an eye or elongating a neck. His judgment of us, his reaction to us, his liking or antipathy, are directly expressed in the drawings which he produced in the Rotonde with unceasing diligence (for there is a very large number of portraits in existence, which are as yet unknown). His drawing was a silent conversation.

If, in the end, all his models look alike, it is in the same way as Renoir's girls. He reduced us all to his type, to the vision within him, and he usually preferred to paint faces, conforming to the physiognomy he required. They possess the superficial resemblance which makes us say that all Chinese or all Japanese look alike, but this is only the means whereby the painter portrays his own image—not the physical appearance, but the mysterious lineaments of his genius; for Modigliani's portraits, even his self-portaits, are not the reflection of his external observation, but of his internal vision, of a vision as gracious, noble, acute and deadly as the fabulous horn of the Unicorn.

As I remember him, on the terrace outside the Rotonde, Modigliani bore no resemblance to those inveterate draftsmen who always have a portfolio under their arm, are always on the lookout for custom and can draw a portrait in a minute. He reminded me rather of the proud, contemptuous gypsies, who sit down at your table and read your hand. But it was the posing of the model that counted; after that, you knew what to expect, and the actual drawing gave you no more information about either the model or the artist. In any case, Modigliani did not paint to order, and he exaggerated his drunkenness, his outbursts of fury and his incongruous laughter as a defence against importunate would-be models, who were offended by his haughtiness.

Towards the end of his tragically short life, he worked harder, shutting himself up at Zborowski's and producing a constant stream of nudes and feminine portraits, which have since made their way all over the world and are beginning to come to rest in museums and galleries.

Many other writers will discuss his qualities as a painter. But he was more than a painter—he was in every sense an artist, and his work is above all the record of the nobility and the singularity of an artist's soul.

(translated by F. A. McFarlane)[1]

[1] Mr. McFarlane's translation was made from an earlier version of the piece on Modigliani which was originally written, as far as I know, as a preface to a collection of reproductions. The contents, however, vary only a little from the text published in *Poésie Critique*, Paris, 1959.

Raymond Roussel

In 1966 Raymond Roussel's difficult novel Impressions of Africa *appeared in English, forty-eight years after it was first published in French. Roussel's public has never been wide, even in France, and the reader who is meeting him now for the first time would benefit from reading Rayner Heppenstall's study* Raymond Roussel *(London, 1966), published when the novel was translated. Mr. Heppenstall makes a particular reference to Cocteau's admiring remarks about Roussel and wonders how Cocteau felt when in 1935 a posthumous essay by Roussel appeared, entitled* How I Wrote Certain of My Books. *Cocteau had always admired what appeared to be genuine, straightforward creative work, hermetic, perhaps, but spontaneous. Roussel's explanation of his method would appear to show that it was synthetic. Cocteau, however, would have remained undaunted: once he admired, or rather loved a writer, nothing would have made him change his mind.*

Raymond Roussel or genius in its pure state, inassimilable for the élite. The passive obedience of the schizophrenic who dwells within us and for whom we merely supply the manpower. *Locus Solus* questions the whole of literature and advises me once more to be wary of admiration and seek out love, which is mysteriously comprehending. In fact even one of the innumerable admirers of the work of Anatole France or Pierre Loti cannot find in them one scrap of genius which atones for their fame if he remains blind to *Locus Solus*. He therefore adopts France or Loti for the reasons that separate us from them.

This proves, alas, that genius is a question of immediate dosage and slow evaporation.

Ever since 1910 I have heard people laugh at the "rails like calves' lights" in *Impressions d'Afrique*. Why should you imagine that the fear of being laughed at touches Roussel? He is alone. If you find him funny, he will prove to you in a few lines (*Olga Tcherwonenkoff*) how his sense of the comic is opposed to his gravely meticulous lyricism.

As a postscript to a letter he sent me recently, he quoted this passage from *Les Mariés de la Tour Eiffel*:[1]

First Loudspeaker: *But this telegram is dead.*
Second Loudspeaker: *It's just because it's dead that every-one understands it.*

This postscript proves that Roussel is not unaware either of what he is or of what is due to him.

Certain words make the public laugh. "Calves' lights" prevents us from seeing the delicate statue that these rails support. In *Orphée*[2] the word "rubber" prevented people from hearing Heurtebise's phrase, "She has forgotten her rubber gloves." When I acted this role I succeeded by means of imperceptible preparations, in reducing and then in suppressing the laughter. The audience were prepared without knowing it and expected the word "rubber" instead of being surprised by hearing it suddenly pronounced. Then they understood the surgical aspect of the term.

Roussel and Proust disprove the legend of the poet's indispensable poverty, his struggle to live, the garrets and the lobbying. Rejection by the various élites, the automatic non-adoption of anything new, is not explained only by the restrictions that a poor man overcomes gradually.

Thanks to his fortune Proust lived shut in with his universe; he could afford the luxury of being ill. He was, in fact, ill because illness was possible; nervous asthma, his ethic in the form of imaginative care for his health, brought on real illness and death.

[1] Cocteau's *comédie-ballet* of 1924.
[2] The play was first produced in 1927, and in one production Cocteau himself played Heurtebise.

Roussel's fortune allows him to live alone and ill without prostituting himself to the slightest extent. His riches protect him. He peoples emptiness. There is not the slightest grease spot on his work. He is a world hung with elegance, fantasy and fear.

In the end *Impressions d'Afrique* leaves an impression of Africa. The story of the Zouave is the only example of writing comparable to a certain type of painting, sought by our friend Uhde,[3] which he calls painting "of the sacred heart."

With the exception of Picasso, in another medium, nobody has made use better of newspaper than Roussel. The judge's cap on *Locus Solus'* head, the brimless cap worn by Romeo and Juliet and Seil-Kor.

The same applies to the atmospheres in which Roussel's imagination moves. Old Casino *décors*, old furniture, old costumes, scenes like those one sees painted on the organs, the fairground booths of the prison, the Decapitator and the Musée Dupuytren.[4] The new is only presented in the guise of the fabulous: the sea-horses and the Sauternes, Faustine, Rhedjed's flight, and Fogar's turn.

I have mentioned a similarity between Roussel and Proust. It is a social and physical similarity between outlines, voices, and nervous habits acquired in the same milieu where they both spent their youth. But the difference between their work is absolute. Proust saw a great number of people. He led a highly complex night life. He found the material for his great timepieces outside. Roussel sees nobody. He finds material only within himself. He even invents historical anecdotes. He operates his automats without the slightest outside help.

Proust, Swann, Gilberte and Balbec always make me think of Souann in *Impressions d'Afrique*, the ancestor of the Talous, and of the phrase in *Locus Solus*: "Gilbert waves over the ruins of Baalbek the famous uneven sistrum of the great poet Missir."

[3] German-born painter, best known for his works on religious themes.
[4] The museum of anatomy in Paris, named after the surgeon Guillaume Dupuytren (1777–1835), who left money for its foundation.

Roussel's style is a means, not an end. It is a means that has become an end beneath the hard cash of genius, for the beauty of his style arises from the fact that he applies himself to saying difficult things with precision, relying only on his own authority, leaving no intriguing shadow around him. But since he is an enigma and *has nothing round about him,* this illumination is much more intriguing.

If Giorgio de Chirico took to writing instead of painting I suppose he would create with his pen an atmosphere similar to that of the Place des Trophées.

When we read the description of this square we think of him.[5]

Under the influence of opium one delights in someone like Roussel and does not attempt to share this pleasure. Opium desocializes us and removes us from the community. Further, the community takes its revenge. The persecution of opium addicts is an instinctive defence by society against an anti-social gesture. I regard these notes on Roussel as the proof of gradual return to a certain reduced communal life. Instead of carrying his books away to my hideout, I would like to spread them abroad. When I smoked opium I was too lazy. One must beware of the downhill path to the communal grave.

It is to Gide, who generously read *Impressions d'Afrique* to us in the past, that I owe the discovery of *Locus Solus* and the recent reading of the admirable *Poussière de Soleils.*

In the eyes of Roussel, *the objects that he transfigures remain what they are.* It is the least artistic genius. It is the acme of art. Satie would say that it was the triumph of the *amateur.*

Roussel's equilibrium is taken for disequilibrium. He hopes for official praise and he knows his work is misunderstood, thereby proving that official praise is not despicable because it is official, but because it is badly exercised.

[5] (1930). *Hebdoméros* proves me right. Chirico has not read Roussel. It is a family likeness. (Author's note.) [Cocteau is referring to Chirico's only "novel," which could be described as a picaresque of the imagination. Tr.]

Roussel shows first of all the end without the means, and he produces surprises which rest on a feeling of security, as in *Le Gala des Incomparables*. These methods embellish the end of his book. But since they embody the strangeness that they owe to the person of the author, they do not weaken the problems that they illuminate and to which they add a new and adventurous luster.

The divinatory episodes which end *Locus Solus* are convincing. Here the author reveals first the experiments and then the devices behind them, but the devices depend on a reality, on Roussel, just as the devices admitted by the conjuror do not make us capable of performing the trick. The conjuror who reveals his trick transfers peoples' minds from a mystery they reject to a mystery they accept, and places to his credit approval which formerly enriched the unknown.

Genius is the farthest extreme of the practical sense.

Everything which logically and practically destines an ordinary object to an unforeseen use, before the slightest automatism or the slightest conscious memory have time to intervene, is genius.

In 1918 I rejected Raymond Roussel as likely to place me under a spell from which I could see no escape. Since then I have built my defences. I can look at him from the outside. (*Opium*, 1930)

Raymond Roussel is reminiscent of that architect-bee, the only one in the hive, if I am not mistaken, who at one glance calculates the building, upside down, of a cathedral which in human terms would be four times as high as the Eiffel Tower. The honey of *Impressions d'Afrique* is delectable, but how little it seems when we have finished the book and can see the nerves, cells and the exquisite, terrible geometry of the whole. *Locus Solus*, where the structure is more hermetic, seems at first to correspond to a theatrical system on Roussel's part: the *enchaînement* system of the Arab rhapsodist. In the end the secret responses and the interlinear idiom make themselves heard and give us gooseflesh, the uneasiness of the Negro tom-tom, when the distant, dark and interminable dialogues begin between invisible tribes of painted insects, their carapaces covered with crossbows and wing-sheaths.

Roussel complained bitterly and naïvely that he was not as famous as Loti. The Academy, the Legion of Honor, all these little dignities fascinated him because in his purity of soul he believed them to be great and still possessing the privileges that they must have had when they began, which in fact they should never have lost. He did not realize that one firm bestows honor while another is degrading. He thought it natural for a poet to pay his publishers. In short he was genuine, really genuine, genuine par excellence, the type of man one does not meet in prison, or in the Foreign Legion or in Marseilles, the official places where really genuine behavior is taught and actually functions. (*En Toute Hâte*, N.R.F., 1933)

I have learned with sorrow that Raymond Roussel is dead. I was proud of his admiration, I mean his friendship, the only form of admiration that I tolerate. I dare not make a choice between two masterpieces like *Impressions d'Afrique* and *Locus Solus*. His dramas enchant us, in the true sense of the term. His last book is perhaps the only volume which we do not know how to approach; it leaps into the memory all at once.

One day when I asked him for the "key" to *Impressions d'Afrique* he replied, "I will explain it after my death."

Has this posthumous exegesis fallen into dutiful hands? I indicate this reply of his, which was so important, and spoken with a grave smile, to those who are grieved by this death. (1933)

Pablo Picasso

*Cocteau has written a great deal about Picasso, from the time of
the early essay included in* Le Rappel à l'Ordre *in 1926. Art critics,
journalists and ex-mistresses have been writing about this prolific
and provocative painter for years and will go on doing so, but
Cocteau's appraisals are different from those of everyone else; they
are sudden spotlights illuminating only the places that* he *chooses
to see and to show to his readers. Others will write about the details of his technique, his sex life, his attitude to money; yet only
Cocteau knows how to combine an unorthodox, apparently lighthearted yet deeply serious interpretation of his painting with telling details, such as how Picasso helped other artists when he first
became successful, plus anecdotes about how visitors to an exhibition reacted to his paintings.*

*This long "essay" is actually a transcript made from an ex-
tempore talk at an exhibition in Rome in 1953.[1] It differs little in
style from much of Cocteau's writing and is an outstanding
example of what he meant by* poésie critique: *an inspired biblio-
graphical term which could probably never be applied to the work
of any other writer. The defects of the genre could be said to
balance its merits with an unhoped-for degree of perfection.*

Forgive me for talking to you impromptu fashion and standing up, but it seems indecent to sit at a table when I'm talking
about a man who lives standing, works standing and hardly ever
sits down.

In Cannes, from the moment he gets up, he knows that the

[1] Published in *La Corrida du Premier Mai*, Editions Bernard Grasset,
1957.

saddle and handle bars of a bicycle are going to turn into an animal's head, that an iron chestnut will turn into a lamp, that he will cast the plaster in bronze and paint the bronze. But dreaming about these things isn't enough, they have to be constructed, and he goes from his bedroom to his studio where his imaginings will take shape. There he devotes himself to incredible operations with plastic metaphors, which means that poetic metaphors, instead of being written down, become visual and can be touched.

At his exhibition in Rome I happened to be near a visitor from abroad who seemed to have an excellent knowledge of painting. He was admiring a bronze monkey. But he hadn't noticed, until I pointed it out to him, that the monkey's face was made up of two little toy motorcars placed one on top of the other. This proved that Picasso was right, and these two superimposed objects had become a third one, that is to say a juxtaposition of unrelated ideas which had assumed a shape.

When I was young and we all lived in Montparnasse, we had no money and no political, social or national problems of any sort. So when people asked me who the great French artists were I was able to reply: Picasso, forgetting he was Spanish, Stravinsky, forgetting he was Russian, and Modigliani, forgetting he was Italian. We formed a group, we fought a lot, we quarreled a lot, but there was a kind of international patriotism among us too. This patriotism is a privilege of Paris and often threatens to make the city incomprehensible to the outsider. But it must never be forgotten that Picasso is Spanish. When he hurls magnificent insults at the human face, they're not really insults. He's insulting the face just as his compatriots insult the Madonna when she doesn't give them what they ask for. Picasso always demands something, and the outside world and matter have to obey him.

When you watch him work you have the impression that like the rest of us he's imprisoned in a very confined space and possesses working tools different from anyone else's. In fact he's a prisoner between four walls, and when I say four walls, our dimensions are unfortunately three and not four.

What does this prisoner do? He draws on the walls. He carves with his knife. If he has nothing to paint with, he paints with blood and fingernails, then he tries to get out of this prison

Picasso and Stravinsky

and starts to attack the walls, which resist, and to bend the bars of his cell. This man is continually struggling with the desire to get out of himself, and when he finishes a piece of work you have the impression that his prison's a jail, and the work an escaping convict, and that it's natural for many people to join the hunt with guns and dogs. But he's also surrounded with the infinite love of people who love liberty and the fact that prisoners do escape.

I'd like to talk to you about the time when we knew each other first. I met Picasso fairly late, in 1916, when he lived in an apartment overlooking the Montparnasse cemetery. It wasn't very cheerful, but he's never cared much about his surroundings, apart from what he can pick up there. For he does pick things up. He's a rag-and-bone man of genius, the king of rag-and-bone men. Whenever he goes out he picks up all the oddments he can find, brings them all back to his studio and raises them to the dignity of usefulness. He doesn't only pick up unusual objects with his hands, but with his eyes too; they notice the slightest thing, and if you study his work carefully you can always recognize the district where he was living when he painted this or that picture, for you can see the elements that inattentive people don't notice: drawings chalked on pavements, shop windows, posters, lampposts spattered with plaster, treasure from dustbins.

Through the first so-called Cubist paintings you can visualize him walking along between the newspaper kiosks and old haberdashers' shops in Montmartre. He uses everything that's old and makes something new, which can cause surprise but fascinates through its realism. Let us understand what we mean by this word realism. Strictly speaking there can't really be any abstract painting, since every painting represents either the painter's ideas or, in the last analysis, the painter himself. Picasso has never claimed to do abstract painting. He searches ferociously for a likeness and finds it in such a way that the object or the face at the origin of his work often loses relief and strength when compared to its representation. Sometimes, when I emerged from the shed where Picasso had been painting *War and Peace,* the outside world would look weak and confused.

For many years the Impressionists believed they were overcoming photography, that photography was a pleonasm which had to be overcome, and it is now more and more apparent that our Impressionists were wonderful color photographers. In the case of Degas, for example, the fact is striking. People have always preferred the thing that a painting represents to the painting itself. Many people think they like painting, but they like the model, the thing that the painter has chosen as a means of expressing himself and as one way, I repeat, of painting his own portrait. Painters can paint a still life, a face or a landscape, but the result is always their own portrait, and here's the proof of it. When you see a Virgin by Raphael, you don't say "The Virgin," you say "Raphael." When you see Vermeer's *Head of a Young Girl,* you don't say "a young girl," but "Vermeer." When you see anemones by Renoir, you don't say "anemones," but "Renoir." And when you see a woman who hasn't an eye where she ought to have one, you don't say, "there's a woman who hasn't an eye where she ought to have one." You say, "Picasso!"

I told you just now that I knew Picasso in 1916. At that time Montparnasse was a provincial place. We seemed to be hanging about there, but we weren't, or rather we were hanging about in the way that young people appear to laze around and do nothing.

There are districts in Paris which rise to the surface. It's the turn of Saint-Germain-des-Prés now. Once it was Montmartre, and in our time (people now call it "the heroic age") Montparnasse had just come up. We wasted time there without doing so, along with Modigliani, Kisling, Lipchitz, Brancusi, Apollinaire, Max Jacob, Blaise Cendrars, Pierre Reverdy, Salmon, all those men who barely understood what they were doing, but who were causing a real revolution in art, literature, painting and sculpture.

This revolution took place in very strange circumstances in the middle of the 1914 war, a war so strange that while we had our posts at the Front we moved backwards and forwards between the Paris front and the fighting front. This is what Apollinaire did, and it wore him out, up to the time of the Armistice when he died, and we thought the town was decorated in his honor and in honor of our artistic patriotism.

This revolution occurred without anyone noticing it, and

when those who might have been alarmed realized what was happening it was too late to fight back. We took advantage of a city which was almost empty, waiting to be captured, and it *was* captured, for ever since that time the work of the men I'm telling you about has never stopped growing in importance.

I'll give you an example of the split between two eras.

When Modigliani did my portrait he was working in the same studio as Kisling, in the rue Joseph-Bara. I don't know what became of the portrait by Kisling in which Picasso can be seen drawing at the back of the room, wearing a black-and-white checked shirt. The Modigliani portrait was painted on a big canvas and he sold it to me for five francs. Unfortunately I hadn't enough money to pay for a cab, which would have allowed me to take the portrait home with me. Kisling owed the Café de la Rotonde eleven francs. He suggested giving this portrait to the proprietor in exchange. The proprietor agreed and the canvas began an odyssey which came to an end when it was sold for seventeen million francs in America.

I'm not telling this anecdote for the sake of complaining and showing that we might have gotten rich and didn't, but to show you how quickly our revolution turned into a regime, which people sometimes hold against it, but it's inevitable.

Another story from the time when Picasso lived in Montmartre. His studio was very untidy, and drawings used to lie scattered about on the floor. One of the first rich collectors came to see Picasso. He bent down, picked up a drawing and asked how much it cost. Picasso replied: "Fifty francs." And when the collector saw there were lots of them, he cried, "Then you've got enough to make a fortune!"

Burglars recently broke into Picasso's apartment in the rue La Boétie and took only linen.

So we occupied Montparnasse, while we carried out this unconscious revolution which, like all revolutions, began in a cellar. Our club used to meet in the little cellar in the rue Huyghens, either to read poems or to play music by the composers who were later called *Les Six*. After this Picasso, who was becoming more famous than his colleagues, and beginning to sell things at high prices, was decent enough to distribute gouaches right and left and then shut his eyes, for he knew very well that his friends would have to sell them. He helped them to live. The myth of Picasso's selfishness is completely untrue. He has always helped friends on the quiet without saying a word about it, and anyone who didn't know this couldn't have known him well.

At the end of 1916 I took Picasso to Rome, where Diaghilev was directing the *Ballets Russes*. Influenced by our reaction to his enterprises, he adopted our group and renewed his ammunition. He had brought only Russian designers to France: Bakst, Alexandre Benois and Larionov. He annexed Picasso, Braque, Derain, Matisse, Laurencin. He tried to annex Renoir, but Renoir was already very old and ailing.

Montparnasse was shocked to see Picasso distort the Aristotelian rules of Cubism and follow me to Rome in order to prepare the ballet *Parade*, to music by Erik Satie.

We told Gertrude Stein about our departure for Rome as though we were announcing an engagement. Taking Picasso to see Diaghilev was like taking Monsieur Renan behind the scenes at a café-concert.

It was the Italian Futurists, led by Marinetti, who helped us. At that time the Futurists consisted of Prampolini, Balla and Carrà. They were kind enough to help us build the frames for Picasso's costumes and to make the work possible. We were convinced that everyone would like our ballet, because we liked the work and we thought it was normal for other people to share our enjoyment. We had no doubt that *Parade*, in 1917, was going to be a great event and a great theatrical scandal. It was given for the first time at the Théâtre du Châtelet, and if the crowd didn't lynch us and tear us apart on the way out, it was only because Apollinaire was wearing a uniform and had been wounded in the head; this wound, which had been anticipated in Chirico's portrait of him, forced him to wear bandages which earned the respect of a naïvely patriotic public. He saved us from the crowd, but only just. As calm was restored after several performances, we heard one gentleman say to another: "If I'd known it was so silly I'd have brought the children."

This remark leads me to quote you the one which must be overheard by so many of Picasso's pictures: "My little boy (or my little girl) could do as well." This is because every master-piece, every major work, looks easy, and if the artists move towards this apparent facility the public turns away from a facility which seems to them false. Unfortunately there is a tendency to prefer anything that affects to be difficult. But anyone who can sense a masterpiece knows that great artists try to be simple. You will object that Picasso's works are not simple. It isn't true. Unlike all the schools of painting, he doesn't go from the infinite to the finite, but always proceeds in a highly elegant fashion, avoiding any aestheticism, from the finite to the infinite, to the non-finished, from perfection to the sketch. If you go through the albums which preceded the preparation of the great fresco *War and Peace*, you will notice that all those faces, all those fighters, dancers, hands and horses have been drawn fifty times over with exact outlines and that gradually, by translating these drawings into paintings, he reached the gigantic sketch which he gave us. He therefore moved in the opposite direction, I repeat, to that which is taught to painters. He began with finished work in order to arrive gradually at an infinite, non-finished work which leaves you room to speculate and dream.

Great politeness which consists of saying to the public: "That's what I offer you, finish it, if you can, in your head or in your heart."

The first question raised by Picasso is always: What does it mean?

The public have been splendidly taken in for several centuries now. They are taken in, because painting is like a distorting mirror which deceives both the eye and the mind. They are shown something which they know already, for they prefer to recognize rather than to learn. Recognition is easier than learning. Many people think they like painting because they recognize shapes they are accustomed to seeing. All at once an extraordinary event occurred. The painter who was mistakenly described as "Cubist," thanks to a witty remark by Matisse, got rid of the pretext. The incident is important, because in the past a building was built with scaffolding, and because after 1912 it could be said that the painter kept only the scaffolding and removed the building, which did not prevent its mass from obtruding in the middle of the scaffolding. Before Picasso, and Braque's gray period, you often have an impression of scaffolding, but the architecture is there beneath it.

Objects follow Picasso as animals followed Orpheus. He takes them wherever he wants, into a despot's kingdom where he has made his own laws. But the objects which follow him always remain recognizable, for Picasso doesn't renounce the idea of strength which dwells in them. An ox's head remains an ox's head. A child remains a child, and Picasso's successive families are as recognizable as those in a family album.

One day, at the Rome exhibition, as I was standing in front of a portrait of Françoise Gilot, I saw a strange sight. An attendant was covering her profile with his cap and saying to a lady: "What can you see?" The lady replied: "A profile." Then he covered the profile and asked: "What do you see now?" "Another profile." It was Françoise's chignon. The attendant then told the lady: "You understand everything." Neither he nor she had understood anything, and nobody needs to understand.

The essential thing is to feel, and try to get inside the mind and actions of a man through whom the attributes of the world travel and acquire strangeness and splendor. It's no paradox to say that Picasso is the first painter who doesn't deceive the public. Apelles deceived even the birds, since they mistook his grapes for real ones.

When our painter tries to escape from his prison, he has moments of relaxation. I won't call it fatigue. He then produces works which are much more attractive than his others. Canvases where the colors are softer, the shapes more pleasing. The portraits of his son Paul illustrate this. There's a halt in the struggle with the canvas which hated being painted on, and covered up; it must think it's being marked, destroyed, soiled. But when Picasso is really himself he takes his realism as far as he can, his own realism which you shouldn't reject just because it's not yours.

The owner of the restaurant Le Catalan confessed to Picasso one day that he didn't understand one of his paintings. Picasso asked him if he understood Chinese. When the restaurant owner replied that he didn't, Picasso said: "It can be learned." And he was right. Conventional art would be unintelligible to a savage. The essential fact is that we've been used to it for a long time, but this doesn't prevent us from breaking away from habit and admitting that art has no need to please or to fly in our faces.

In the Pavillon de Flore at the Louvre I've noticed how many visitors linger in front of the paintings and try to decipher a language. It's a mistake to believe that the artist should give way to the public. It's fairer for the public to give way to the artist, unlike the radio which trickles into houses like warm water from a tap and does what it's told. I'm convinced that if people could hear real music at home, they would accept it and soak themselves in it, they'd get tired of pop singers and realistic female vocalists.

Picasso never gives way to anyone. He has asserted himself through a lofty attitude. Even if he adopts a political family he renounces none of his prerogatives. The way I've known him is the way he'll be until his death, if death dares to interrupt him.

Make no mistake about it, Cubism was a classical phase after the romanticism of the Fauves. This is why the Cubists, to the great surprise of everyone, set up Ingres in opposition to Delacroix, while young people regarded Delacroix as a revolutionary and Ingres as an academic painter. The Cubists had the honor of discovering that young people had been wrong in responding to the ardor of Delacroix while despising the remarkable distortions and the unobvious, incredible audacities of Monsieur Ingres.

Gradually, Picasso has evolved, since he is a movement and not a school. His tornado-like progress brought him to *War and Peace*, in which he celebrated the marriage between *Le Bain Turc* and Delacroix's *Entry of the Crusaders into Constantinople*. Naturally there is nothing in the work resembling either picture, but there is a marriage between a calm strength and an aggressive strength. The result is the astonishing frieze which looks like a sketch and embodies a long meditation originating in *Guernica*.

I'm not unaware that the Picasso tornado represents a danger for youth. This danger comes from the fact that he triple-locks every door he opens. If you tried to follow him you would come up against a door. But he represents a hope, because he proves that individualism is not threatened with death and that art rebels against an ideal fit only for termites. Isn't it strange that a man whose art is hermetic should have become as famous as Victor Hugo, whose art is accessible? The young people of today probably think further and try to find subterfuges which can eject their darkness into full daylight.

There is never any distortion or caricature in Picasso's work. There is intensity. Work precedes research. He finds first and searches afterwards. The disparate nature of his work upsets a long-standing habit and a long-standing laziness which have let it be understood that a work is only beautiful by function of its unity. Only this unity must not be a surface unity. Picasso has been my master and that of many men of my generation because he taught us to pay no attention to unity of surface, not to be afraid of being taken for a juggler or an acrobat, of not striking always in the same place and producing exactly the same sound. With each new work I produce I have to make my debut once more and start all over again.

You will argue that our names help us. Sometimes young people say to me: "You're lucky, you can do what you like." Then I recount the obstacles in our way, obstacles caused by our names, for everyone wants us to repeat our posthumous successes and they reproach us for turning our backs on them. We are indebted to Picasso for this method of achieving freshness, this insistence that we should not be recognized by our costumes, and that our look alone gives us away. I will tell you one of Picasso's greatest secrets: He runs faster than beauty. This is why his creations look ugly. I will explain myself: A man who runs more slowly than beauty will produce flabby works; a man who runs at the same speed as beauty will produce flat works; a man who runs faster than beauty will make it breathless and force it to catch up with his work, and in the end *his* work will become beautiful. There is nothing more fatal than running side by side with beauty or lagging behind it. You must get ahead of it, exhaust it, make it ugly. And it is this exhaustion which makes new beauty as magnificently ugly as the Medusa's head.

Forgive me for speaking to you disjointedly. It's difficult to follow an itinerary with a man who says that beauty is a job for the blind. He told me that he once saw in Avignon an old near-blind painter painting the Palace of the Popes. The old painter's wife was standing beside him, looking at the Palace through binoculars and describing it to him. The painter followed his wife's descriptions. Picasso follows nobody's descriptions but only what he tells himself about what he has seen. This is what endows his work with an immediate and incomparable imaginative power.

There's a darkness within each one of us that we don't know very well or don't know at all. This darkness wants to emerge, but at the same time doesn't want to. This is the drama of art, a real struggle between Jacob and the angel. And, except when he makes pottery to keep his hands from being idle, I don't think Picasso has ever created anything without being the victim of a terrifying struggle with himself.

Frederick Nietzsche speaks of men-mothers, those men who continually give birth and escape the critical approach because the creative spirit devours them. This might have been a prophetic portrait of Picasso and, what is more, like all great creators, he's both man and woman at the same time: a strange marriage. I don't think there's ever been so much crockery smashed in any other household.

In 1916 he wanted to paint my portrait in Harlequin costume. This portrait turned out to be a Cubist painting in which I couldn't possibly be recognized. After the sittings we used to walk around Montparnasse and go up to see the painters. They would bolt their doors and didn't open them until they had hidden their pictures in cupboards. "He'll use my way of painting trees," they would say, or "He'll take the siphon I've put in the painting away from me." They attached great importance to the slightest detail, and the reason why Picasso's colleagues were afraid of him coming to see them was because they knew that his eyes were going to see everything, swallow everything, assimilate everything and reconstruct it all in his work with a richness of which they were incapable.

People approve or disapprove of Picasso, but he still intrigues the world, a world which logically should no longer take any interest in art and consider it as a luxury.

Picasso's great friends, apart from myself, have been Apollinaire, André Salmon, Max Jacob, Gertrude Stein, Pierre Reverdy and Paul Eluard. Poets. Isn't it significant that Picasso prefers to live with poets rather than with painters? For he is a great poet. His paintings express and reflect the same demands as our poems. His syntax is visual, comparable to a writer's syntax. It looks as though each of his pictures tries to respond to what Guillaume Apollinaire called the event poem.When he comes up against a new syntax, that is, a series, one canvas out of this series always crowns it with success, sums it up and becomes an event.

Let us return to Montparnasse. Our group dissolved with the birth of Surrealism. The Dada movement (Tristan Tzara–Arp –Marcel Duchamp–Picabia–Ribemont Dessaigne) preceded the Surrealist team consisting of Breton, Eluard, Aragon, Desnos, Max Ernst, Dali, Miró, Masson, Paul Klee, and so on. Chirico is determined to deny his role in it. The Surrealists hadn't been given this name yet. We quarrelled almost at once because I didn't want to take orders. Surrealism proceeded by edicts. I'm a free man; I've always been free, and I shall remain so until the end. After quarrelling with the Surrealists I defended the same causes as they did, but I worked alone, while they worked in a group. They annexed Picasso, and the thing that proves this man's style is the fact that he never espoused our quarrel, which lasted seventeen years, and this quarrel never caused a rift between us. Gradually we all became reconciled, I became a great friend of Eluard and then unfortunately I lost him. A great friend of Eluard and a great friend of all those with whom I had fought, no doubt because it had to be so.

The style of discord has changed. Politics have assumed great importance. Some went to the right, others to the left. We are no longer familiar with that attitude which allowed me to have Picasso as a master while accepting at the same time the influence of an old man and a boy–Erik Satie and Raymond Radiguet.

If you have only seen pictures of Picasso, I should like to describe him to you. He is very small, with delightful feet and hands, and terrible gimlet eyes which bore right through the outside and the inside. Intelligence trickles out of him like water from the rose of a watering can. You can sometimes be chilled by this cold spray, but you always benefit from it. His cutting words often go beyond what he intends to say. It rarely happens

77

that you don't think about them the next day and learn from them, and that his clairvoyance, which is full of grace and harshness, doesn't dictate some of our own discipline over ourselves. Otherwise he likes formulas. I once said that he had brought his terra-cotta doves to life by wringing their necks. He liked this remark, for he himself uses formulas all the time. He doesn't talk, he formulates. His lyricism never pours out, it's never torrential. It gathers itself together and assumes the shape of sculptured objects which you can walk around and touch, which owe their effectiveness to an interior illumination.

I thought I was going to talk to you in particular about Picasso's friends, and I realize that I've talked about something quite different. But isn't this a way of paying homage to a painter who has always started out without knowing where he was going and whose arrival, in the end, is a triumph? There isn't time and I couldn't find the words to tell you by what process he changes his rhythm on the way. A piece of torn paper lying on the floor could do it, as happens in the case of thoroughbred horses whose jockeys whip them when they rear. But this would take us into a domain where the friendly impromptu talk I'd promised you would lose its real significance.

Let it suffice that I have acknowledged the Pope, the Borgia of a church in which the doomed painters, with Van Gogh at their head, were the first martyrs.

Pierre Loti

Most of the portraits in this collection have a Parisian background,
usually Montmartre or Montparnasse, while Cocteau's early home
in the rue d'Anjou figures in some of them. In other pieces we
can catch glimpses of Provence, the Bassin d'Arcachon or the
Côte d'Azur. Paris is the background inseparable from Cocteau's
early life at least, and he has always been more preoccupied with
the human landscape than with what are usually called "travel
pictures." But there is one unexpected picture in his portrait
gallery which proves delightfully what happened when Cocteau
traveled, and how his technique transcended any transplantation
of subject matter.

This imaginary re-creation of Pierre Loti, whom Cocteau had
met when he was young, is a cheerful and moving fantasy-
evocation of the unhappy but outwardly highly respectable
Frenchman who lived from 1850 to 1923 and, through Pêcheur
d'Islande, Madame Chrysanthème, *etc., became a classic for a*
time. For many people the "painted China goat" may well be a
more enduring image of Loti than formal photographs of the
bearded naval officer whose novels we read at school.

Saturday, 30th April, 1949

This morning I wanted to go to Eyoub. As we came through
the Bosphorus, I noticed the house where Loti lived and also the
other one to which Anna de Noailles was brought as a little girl
by the Princesse de Brancovan. Far from France, we are moved
by these things. In Paris, which respects no one, they would be
made fun of. Pierre Loti and Anna de Noailles have been thrown
on the scrap heap. It's a great mistake. The Turks remember
them. Loti's faint aroma, submerged by the revolution, now rises

79

again and is felt like sweet scent on the cemetery hill. Loti is honored at Eyoub as Alphonse Daudet is at Tarascon. The little café, the wooden hut, the "isba" (everything is Russian here, both *isba* and trappings) where Loti came to drink raki and eat yoghurt sandwiches, all remain untouched above the level of reformations and new factories.

"Piyer Loti—Kir-Gazinosu." Above the tombs, the factories and the lovely meanderings of the Golden Horn, the little eyrie bears an inscription with this strange spelling. But the tombs don't stop at the foot of the hill—don't you believe it! They only form the spring for a river of tombs which submerge everything. The mosques are tombs, the public buildings are tombs, and the gardens also are tombs and Istanbul is a cemetery full of tombs where the living, according to Mohammedan fashion, live and eat on tombs.

What struck me most in the courtyard of the Eyoub mosque was a gigantic Byzantium plane tree, full of nests where herons breed and from which pigeons cover the ground with their droppings. The tree is hollow and the hole in it makes a sort of cavern which has been fitted with a red door. There any injured or sick herons are enclosed and cared for. Cats come here and play about at the foot of the tree. Old women, wrapped up in black, wring the necks of cocks which they carry by their claws strung together. Until the moment they are killed, the cocks try to pick up grain dropped by the pigeons on to the courtyard tiles. These old women crouch down, and when they rise up awkwardly one thinks at first that they must have been passing water, but it is cock's blood which wets the tiles. When I knew Loti he was like one of the herons which we see in the tree. Balanced on his Louis XV heels, his nose covered with powder and his eyes looking like the buttons on his little boots.

What a journey up to his eyrie! The car refuses to go farther. For the last ten minutes it has been climbing roads which no one should go up except on a donkey. We are knocking against barrows of oranges and onions. Arabs would be screaming and threatening. The Turks display no anger. Everyone gives the chauffeur plenty of advice.

It is so difficult to get along that discussions sound more as if they came from players excited over a difficult move. We emerge from the passageways as the result of group deliberations. The hill, however, with its cobbles and steep inclines, is too much for the car, which stops dead after a few shakes and hiccups.

We continue the climb on foot between the tombstones and a few cypresses left standing by the soldiers who came here in 1914. The tombstones lean drunkenly to one side, knocked over in all directions like clothes stands holding up a stone turban, a stone fez, stone flowers for the ladies and more complicated headdresses for the eunuchs.

Charming Loti! I can imagine him skipping down this rocky hillside looking like a painted china goat. With his little tight corsets, his little high-heeled shoes, his little painted face, his large moustache, his staring eyes, I can hardly see him meeting some Azyadé, as ambiguous as Proust's young girls. But after all, are not these young girls full of the same charm as Calderon's caricatures of horsemen? From so much dreaming, effort and interplay of feelings, there remains nothing but a graceful platform from which we can gaze down at the most fabled failure of human effort. A piled-up mass of empires, glamorous luxury, massacres, conquests, strongholds of vainglory destroyed by earth-quakes, a labyrinth of races and beliefs, lust for possession, destruction and contrariness, tombs, tombs, tombs . . . all these combine to form an inextricable amphitheater of boxes and chandeliers where dead centuries pile up in front of a proscenium of water.

Cocteau came to visit Loti's house during his tour of Egypt and the Middle East in 1949 when a theatrical company, which included Yvonne de Bray and Jean Marais, presented a group of French plays, ranging from Racine and Feydeau to La Machine Infernale. The theatrical atmosphere runs through these pages about Loti, culminating with a "curtain" that is nothing short of cataclysmic.

The account which Cocteau wrote of the tour, Maalesh, was published in France in 1949, and in England (Peter Owen Ltd.) and the United States (Hillary House), translated by his friend Mary C. Hoeck, in 1956.

Charlie Chaplin

Cocteau's contribution to the cinema has been so stimulating for so many people, even in the case of some films which I, at least, shall always consider bad, that it would have been a pity if all mention of film personalities had been excluded from this anthology through lack of material. Fortunately, in Mon Premier Voyage *(translated by W. J. Strachan in 1958 as* My Journey Round the World*) there is a delightfully relaxed picture of Charlie Chaplin, whom Cocteau met in 1936 on the* S.S. Coolidge *somewhere between Hong Kong and Shanghai, while going round the world, like Phileas Fogg, in eighty days. His "Passepartout" was Marcel Khill.*

It is always encouraging to find unexpected testimony that corroborates one's own experiences: Cocteau and Chaplin prove here that if one feels affinity with someone all languages dissolve into speech—one can hold a creative conversation in a tongue which is usually incomprehensible, and emerge hours later enriched and gay.

This description of Chaplin hardly dates at all. There is so much bitterness in the film world, especially in the ambiance of Cocteau, that it is a relief to read a few pages about it where there are no signs of strife.

Two poets follow the straight line of their destiny. It suddenly happens that these two lines intersect, forming a cross, or if you prefer, a star. My meeting with Charlie Chaplin remains the delightful miracle of this voyage. So many people have planned this meeting for us, tried to be its organizers. But on each occasion some obstacle arose and now chance—which poets know by another name—throws us together on an ancient Japanese cargo boat, transporting merchandise on the China seas between Hong Kong and Shanghai.

Charlie Chaplin is on board. It is a staggering piece of news. Later on Chaplin was to say: "The real function of a person's work is to make it possible for friends like ourselves to cut out preliminaries. We have always known each other." But up to that moment I had no idea that the wish was mutual. Furthermore this voyage had taught me how capricious fame was. I had had, it is true, the pleasure of finding myself translated into all languages, but in some places where I expected friendship I had met with a blank; elsewhere I expected a blank and had been overwhelmed with friendship. I decided to write Chaplin a short note. I mentioned my presence on board and my affection for him. He came down to his dinner table with Paulette Goddard. His manner conveyed to me that he desired to preserve his incognito.

The truth of the matter was that my letter had not been handed to him. He did not know that I was on board and did not connect me with the table companion whom he could only half see. After dinner I returned to my cabin. I was undressing when I heard a knock at my door. I opened it. It was Charlie and Paulette. My note had just been delivered. Chaplin was afraid it might be a joke or a trap. He had hurried off to ask for a passenger list from the purser, and then sure of his facts, decided to run down and reply in person.

No response could have been simpler nor more youthful. I was touched. I begged them to go and wait for me in their cabin and just give me time to slip on a dressing-gown and pass the news on to Passepartout, who was writing in the reading-room.

You can imagine the innocence, the violent and fresh impact of this extraordinary meeting for which our horoscopes alone had been responsible. I was meeting a myth in flesh and blood. Passepartout's eyes devoured his childhood's hero. Chaplin shook his white curls, removed his glasses, put them back, gripped my shoulders, burst out laughing, turned to his companion and kept repeating, "Isn't it marvelous? Isn't it marvelous?" I do not speak English; Chaplin does not speak French. Yet we talked without the slightest difficulty. What is happening? What is this language? It is *living* language, the most living of all, and springs from the

83

will to communicate at all costs in the language of mime, the language of poets, the language of the heart. Chaplin detaches every word, stands it on the table, as it were, on a plinth, walks back a step, turns it where it will catch the best light. The words he uses for my benefit are easily transported from one language to the other. Sometimes the gesture precedes the words and escorts them. He announces each word first before pronouncing it and comments on it afterwards. No slowness, or only the apparent slowness of balls when a juggler is juggling with them. He never confuses them; you can follow their flight in the air.

The ingenuous Las Cases, writing in his *Memoirs* about the Emperor Napoleon's bad English, comments: "From this combination of circumstances was born a veritably new language."

It was certainly a new language that we were talking, that we brought to perfection and to which we stuck, to everybody's surprise. This language was comprehended only by the four of us, and when they reproached Paulette, who speaks French well, for not coming to our rescue, she replied, "If I help them, they will lose themselves in details. Left to their own devices, they only say the essentials." A remark which speaks volumes for her intelligence.

A necessary reserve stops me from telling you Chaplin's projects in detail. Precisely because he opened his heart to me I find it impossible to hand this wealth over to the public. What I am at liberty to say is that it is his dream to film the Crucifixion in the middle of a dance hall where no one notices it. His Napoleon was to be a fantasy of the Elba period (a comic-opera Napoleon). From now on Chaplin is going to renounce "Charlie." "I am the most exposed of men," he said. "I work in the street. My aesthetics are those of a kick in the pants, and I am beginning to get it back." A remarkable statement and one which sheds light on one whole aspect of his character. In the modern jargon, he is suffering from a vast inferiority complex. It is equaled only by his rightful pride and a system of reflexes suitable for defending his solitude (which he finds painful) and allowing no one to encroach on his prerogatives.

Even friendship is suspect—the duties and inconveniences it entails. His instant taking to me was, it seems, unique, and it produced a kind of panic in him. I felt him withdraw into himself again, and close up after his expansiveness.

He is making his next film, in which he himself is not appearing, for Paulette. He is to shoot three episodes of it at Bali. He is busy with the script and never stops writing. He recites the dialogues to me. This film seems to be a kind of halt before a new cycle. But can he ever take leave of his "poor Pagliacci" theme, removed from the commonplace though it be by his genius? His next role is to be that of a clown torn between the contrasts of real life and the "boards." How carefully he restricts himself to this facile, sentimental ballad theme, which he redeems from banality by his attention to detail so that the most easily satisfied as well as the most solid audience could follow his progress on the tight rope.

I ought to have guessed that *Modern Times* was a terminal work by this sign; for the first time at the end of the film Charlie *does not walk off alone* down the road.

In any case Charlie was gradually shedding the type as he became the individual. The moustaches got smaller, the boots shorter. If he is to take character parts, let us hope that one day he will give us Dostoevski's *The Idiot*. Is not Prince Myshkin a hero after his own heart?

I spoke to him about *The Gold Rush* being one of those gifts in an artist's life. A work that seemed to have a blessed life from start to finish, to walk on a ridge of snow poised halfway between earth and heaven. I saw that my description was an accurate one and that he does indeed reserve a special place in his work for *The Gold Rush*. "The dance of the bread rolls! That's what they all congratulate me on. It is a mere cog in the machine. A detail. If that was what they specially noticed they must have been blind to the rest!"

I remember that charming incident, that farce invented to dazzle the guests, that faculty for flying in one's dreams and imagining that one will be able to teach others how to do it, and that one will still be able to fly when one wakes.

He is right; those who praised and mentioned only this particular item failed to understand this love epic, this *chanson de geste*. It is a film finely balanced between life and death, waking and sleeping; it is the candlelight of sad Christmases. In it Chaplin lowers, as it were, the brothers Williamson's diving bell to the depths of his nature. He turns over the pages in his flora and fauna of the great depths. In the cabin episode he combines the popular legends of the North with the chicken episode which is pure Greek comedy and tragedy.

"One hasn't always the luck to produce a work that grows like a tree every time. *The Gold Rush, A Dog's Life, The Kid* are exceptional. I worked too long on *Modern Times.* When I had worked a scene up to perfection, it seemed to fall from the tree. I shook the branches and sacrificed the best episodes. They existed in their own right. I could show them separately, one by one, like my early one-reelers."

He mimed the cut scenes. He set his *décor* in the narrow cabin, directed his supers, played his own part. We shall never forget the scene in which he incites a town to revolt and holds up all the traffic on account of a piece of wood that he is trying to thrust into the gutter with his little cane.

Paulette went off for a few minutes. Charlie bent over and whispered in a mysterious voice, "And then I feel such pity." What? Pity for this thousand-spiked cactus, this little lioness with her mane and superb claws, this great sports Rolls with its shining leatherwork and metal? The whole of Chaplin is in that remark; that is what his heart is like.

Pity for himself, the tramp, pity for us, pity for her—the poor waif whom he drags after him to make her eat because she is hungry, to put her to bed because she is sleepy, to snatch her away from the snares of city life because she is pure. And suddenly I no longer see a Hollywood star in her silver satin page-boy outfit nor the rich impresario with his white curls and salt-and-pepper tweeds—but a pale little man, curly-haired, with his comic cane, dragging away a victim of the ogre of capital cities and police-traps, as he stumbles along through the world on one leg.[1]

---

[1] He owes his good fortune to the fact that his sympathy is his natural bent, whereas it usually diverts us from ours, and that the practice of his pity carries it on to its goal instead of spoiling and weakening it. (Author's note.)

Chaplin is your good child who puts out his tongue as he works.

It was a child who came down to my cabin, a child who invited us to California, and it is a couple of children who after the filming of *Modern Times* decided on a five-minute impulse to set off for Honolulu, travel around the world hand in hand.

I find it extremely difficult to fit the two pictures together. The florid-complexioned man who is talking to me and the pale little ghost who is his multiple angel, whom he can divide up like quicksilver. I gradually succed in superimposing the two Chaplins. A grimace, a wrinkle, a gesture, a wink and the two silhouettes coincide, that of the fool of the Bible, the little saint in a bowler hat who tugs at his cuffs and straightens his shoulders as he enters paradise, and that of the impresario pulling his own strings.

One evening he asked me to lend him Passepartout. He wanted to turn him into the star of the Bali film. He had been looking for the right man and had found him. Passepartout would be the ideal partner for Paulette, etc., etc. You can imagine Passepartout's excitement. Alas, it was our fault that the scheme could not be realized, for the sole condition was that Passepartout should learn English in England in the next three months, a tour de force which he had made up his mind to accomplish but which circumstances and my work rendered impossible.

The fact remained, however, that Passepartout had encountered his "fateful moment on the high seas" as the fortune-teller had once predicted, which proves that young men should travel out and meet their fate halfway.

The miracle, as Passepartout said, without a hint of bitterness, was that Chaplin should offer him the part. The luxury of his position was that he could not accept it. It changed his life into a fairy tale.

The project strengthened our bonds and brought us closer together. We joined forces, shared our meals and the journey alike; to such an extent did we form the habit of living together that we found it painful to part company at San Francisco.

Our encounter was not just a meeting of two artists full of

curiosity about each other. We were sworn brothers, finding and understanding each other.

When Chaplin is working on a film, whether he locks himself up in his cabin or paces up and down his studio, he is completely absorbed in the job in hand. He takes his fear of being distracted from it to the point of rejecting life and confining himself within some simple problems and exhausting their possibilities. An old man's smile, a Chinese mother suckling her newborn baby, some detail observed in the poor quarter are all grist to his mill. He does not look any further and shuts himself up in his beloved work.

"I don't like work," said Paulette.

Chaplin loves it; and as he loves Paulette he makes work of that. The rest of life bores him. As soon as you distract him from his work, he becomes weary, yawns, stoops, his eyes lose their sparkle. He plunges into somnolence.

Chaplin should be pronounced in the French way, like the painter's family.

Two things about his ancestry are a source of pride to him; his French descent and his gypsy grandmother.

In physical and moral make-up, the little man of the films comes from the Jewish quarter. His bowler hat, overcoat, shoes, curly hair, his pity, his proud yet humble soul are the flower of the ghetto. Is it not a significant and admirable thing that Chaplin's favorite painting is Van Gogh's *The Old Shoe*?

12th May

Charlie is working.

Shut up in his cabin for the last two days, unshaven, in a suit which is too tight, his hair untidy, he stands fidgeting his glasses in those very small hands of his, setting in order sheets of paper covered with writing.

"I might get drowned bathing tomorrow," he confided to me at Shanghai. "*I* do not count. I don't exist. Only this paper exists and counts."

Rendezvous at Hotel Cathay at five p.m. Dinner that reunites businessmen who have come from Hollywood.

All the time at table Charlie yawns. In this dance hall which is Chinese but is doing its best not to look so, only one plank of the floor speaks of China, and on it we are to see an artiste who sums up this squalid town—Shanghai where Lili Marlene would not find room to move and could only be *European*—sitting at the *Venus* under a bluish trellis among the "taxi girls" (the name for girls of every race with whom you dance in exchange for a ticket—five for a dollar).

"The White Flower of Chinatown" was how Marlene Dietrich described herself, speaking into a boa of cockerel feathers. It is difficult to imagine this flower, in this cracked vase in which the flowers cannot be less than two nights old, on a dance floor.

Look at this pitiable dance which Charlie watches open-mouthed, with his double chin resting on his tie and his brow furrowed with crow's-feet. A poor redhead with her hair done like a female clown surmounted with a chimney sweep's hat, with one leg bare, the other in a pierrot's trousers, a checkerboard between her thighs, gloves with red spangles, embarks on the first notes of Debussy's *Cakewalk*.

Picture to yourself this dimly lit stage surrounded by gowned Chinese who provide us with an exhibition of theological students dancing the tango, Chinese girls and half-castes hoping to be taken for patronesses, and under this spotlight, accompanied by an orchestra with gilt music stands and green lanterns, this woman saying to herself, "I am going to invent a modern number, an acrobatic dance, which will be a hotch-potch of our time, plus Pierrot's melancholy, a clown's antics, grimaces of the devil, the agility of a ship's boy and the provocativeness of a vamp." And off she goes, leaping, falling with her toes turned in, putting out her tongue, sinking her head into her shoulders, making eyes, clawing the air, wagging an admonitory finger, pouting, pirouetting, hopping on one foot, rolling her hips, surveying the horizon under her raised hand and pulling on imaginary ropes—in short, all the usual routine.

This wretched woman sums up a Shanghai of which you get a front view when you try to interrupt the wild dash of one-eyed coolies, who only last four years and gallop full pelt straight ahead without knowing where they are going.

The guests at the dance café rise to their feet and revolve on the floor. Chaplin remains at the table. He is ruminating. The people who look at him, trying to place him, are causing him visible embarrassment.

I have left him to himself. Some of my compatriots wanted me to join them at their table. He is sulking. He stretches over from his table to tell me about a cockfight in Spain. The impresario of the fight, a colossus with the hands of a marchioness, little dumpy white hands, the palms of which he rubs gently, voluptuously, in the blood. No other movement except a flutter of these fine hands and a slight quiver of his nostrils.

Suddenly Paulette gets up. She would like to "see Shanghai." But there is nothing to see. But it has to be "done." My French friends give me to understand that there is a secret Shanghai. They are racking their brains. Chaplin is returning to the hotel to sleep. He is going back to stow his fountain pen and camera safely away, precious machines from which the ink and images might escape, and it is important for them to be wrapped up in cotton wool for the night.

One more glimpse of him in Yokohama:

We catch sight of little Charlie Chaplin and little Paulette Goddard who are coming on board. Solemn sirens send out their appeal. Charlie Chaplin shakes himself free from the journalists. With his felt hat put on sideways—Napolean Bonaparte style, one hand in his waistcoat, the other behind his back—this lonely figure, who is too much at home everywhere to be at home anywhere, climbs up the gangway and gets away with a final pirouette.

And the last glimpse of each other:

Last day on the *Coolidge*. The cricket is singing its head off. We meet ladies in their traveling clothes which make them unrecognizable. Charlie Chaplin has the same expression as mine, the long face of a child on the verge of tears. It is the end of a very intimate friendship. Chaplin is returning to Los Angeles; I am going back to Paris. But each of us now knows that the other exists, how his mind works, and "that," says Charlie, "is a good thing."

Edith Piaf

If Chaplin was so international that he had no country of his own, Edith Piaf was so French that she took the essence of France wherever she went. Her unique art, almost perhaps an art form in itself, survives to some extent in her records and the book she wrote about herself. Cocteau appreciated her theatrical genius in all its phases, understanding her so well that nobody else perhaps could ever do justice to the monologues he wrote for her, such as Le Bel Indifférent or Le Fantôme de Marseilles, minor masterpieces which can still fascinate the reader.

In writing this introduction to her book Au Bal de la Chance, Cocteau completed his portrait of her, one for which he had already made various sketches. As we read the description which compares her to the nightingale, we are inevitably reminded of another woman whose genius was theatrical, although she never appeared on the stage: the Comtesse de Noailles. Cocteau so loved his "sacred monsters" that he drew them close to himself, so close that in many ways they all began to resemble each other.

I admire the freedom with which Stendhal uses the word "genius." He finds genius in a woman as she steps into a carriage; in a woman's smile; in a card-player who allows his opponent to win. He rescues it from the abstract and clothes it with meaning. This means that in these women and in this card-player are to be seen all those qualities that are the epitomization of charm and grace. And so, when I say that Madame Edith Piaf has genius, I am borrowing from Stendhal. She is unique. There has never been another like her . . . and there never will be! Like Yvette Guilbert or Yvonne George, like Rachel or Réjane, she burns brightly in the nocturnal solitude of the skies of France. And this star is the symbol for those romantics who still know how to love, how to suffer and how to die.

Look at her, this little woman; look at her hands . . . those tenacious, lizard-like hands. Her forehead is Napoleonic; her eyes are full of wonder . . . eyes which have known blindness and now see again. What will her voice be like? How will she express herself? This tiny person . . . how will she project the powerful laments of night? And then . . . she sings, or, like the April nightingale, she ventures the first notes of her song of love.

Have you ever heard the nightingale? She strains. She hesitates. She grates. She chokes. Her voice rises and falls again. And then, suddenly, she sings. You are captured.

Like the nightingale, Edith Piaf explores herself and her audience; quickly, she finds her voice. In the voice is the whole of the woman; it unfolds itself like a wave of black velvet. This wave of warmth submerges us . . . wraps itself around us. The illusion is complete. Edith Piaf, like the invisible nightingale on her branch, becomes invisible. We are aware only of her eyes, her pale hands, that waxen forehead which reflects the light, and the voice. The voice swells and climbs and, almost unnoticeably, takes the place of the singer. From this moment, the genius of Madame Edith Piaf is seen and acknowledged by all. She surpasses herself and she surpasses her songs. She surpasses the music and the words . . . and us! The soul of the street filters into every room in the town. It is no longer Madame Edith Piaf who sings . . . it is the rain that falls . . . it is the wind that blows . . . it is the moon as she spreads her mantle of light.

La bouche d'ombre—this very phrase seems to have been invented for her oracular mouth.[1]

(translated by P. Trewartha and A. Masoin de Virton)

[1] This introduction appeared in *The Wheel of Fortune,* the English title of the autobiography of Edith Piaf, published by Chilton Book Company, 1966.

Jean Marais

One actor more than any other is identified with Cocteau the film-maker: Jean Marais, whose acting in L'Eternel Retour, La Belle et la Bête, Les Parents Terribles, L'Aigle à Deux Têtes *and* Orphée *earned him world-wide fame. The following article which Cocteau wrote about him makes interesting references to his stage acting in French classical drama, revealing a different aspect of his art. And, as always, we learn a good deal about Cocteau himself.*

Jean Marais belongs to a caste that is dwindling, one where the Baudelairean-type commitment lies in physical presence.

As a result he can reach only the solitary individuals who make up the mass. Moreover, the prizes he wins, like mine, in France, China, Sweden, Portugal and the United States, are never awarded by a jury but by plebiscites.

Young people find it easier to opt for some directive which is given to them and prevents them from thinking. In Holland, where I was presenting *Orphée*, a young man told us that the film had the drawback of "making people think." You can see how much fear is revealed by such a remark, if it means penetrating into your own mind.

I do not claim to regard Marais as perfect. He is an amalgam. The alcohols he produces are all of the highest quality. Life blends them, shakes them up and dilutes them. If they taste bitter it is because there is no sickly sweetness in them.

His virtue lies in the fact that he has applied to the profession of actor the rules that govern that of the poet. If he accuses himself of showing-off, this is through a regard for scruple and, no doubt, because he finds that showing-off is something that puts down deep roots and cannot leave a man who is continually in the public eye.

An actor cannot wait. He takes advantage, *en passant*, of the privilege of longevity possessed by artistic creations. And no doubt the works take advantage of the actor, operating like plants, with numerous ruses, and constructing traps of scents and colors.

An actor will bring ink to life. His appeal to the public is through their senses, for they are mystified by nature and regard his obstinate attempts to perpetuate the species as a luxury.

However, as far as he can avoid it, Marais does not fall into that type of showing-off that contaminates the world of the stage. He does not scorch himself against the footlights. He blazes. Christian Bérard tried to put out this blaze by ingenious methods, alleging that it resembled "Otéro's diamond corselet,"[1] distracted the eye, upset the ensemble and even did harm to the text. He forgave its use in the role of Néron,[2] for the part, which is rather small, has to shine at the center of the tragedy and last during its moment of eclipse.

Although Marais pleads guilty, I confirm that he lacks the showing-off which is indispensable for convincing crowds immediately and that the showing-off for which he blames himself arises from the occult necessities which cannot be so described.

I should like to follow him in this pursuit with the precise flow of words used by radio commentators, and I regret that our critics do not possess their exactitude. I listen to them as I listen to Albine at the end of *Britannicus*. They bring us invisible events, as she does. Their utterances, like hers, become heated to the point of lyricism when there is competition. They express themselves in terms resembling numbers which allow nothing vague.

I wish I had the ease of Georges Briquet to follow Marais in his race. Unfortunately it is run over distances and tracks which are not very well known.

[1] A well-known French actress.

[2] In Racine's tragedy *Britannicus*, involving the Emperor Nero and his mother Agrippina.

When an underwater fisherman has gone down below sixty feet, he bursts open. Few men, apart from psychiatrists, take the risk of venturing into the darkness of psychology. But let us try all the same to go some way down into it.

Mademoiselle Chanel said that "fashion creates beauty which becomes ugly and art creates ugliness which becomes beautiful." How comical those people are who try to find the counterpart to art in fashion.

The actor has everything to fear from a rapid popularity which degrades him to the level of fashion and detaches him from the works to which he should be allied. We have seen famous actresses who appear only in mediocre works and excel in them just like virtuosi who make use of musical creations instead of serving them. Their *brio* objects to unpromising beauties.

Jean Marais clings to unpromising beauties. His instinct makes him opposed to the chorus, the *vox populi*, the verdict of the élites. But his fear of *brio* is out of step with the profession he represents, the profession which imprisons light and does not allow what the cinema calls false shades of color, such as a cloudy sky. He makes up for this by using thunderbolts, and their dazzling light is propitious for him. This is why he leaps so quickly from reserve to outbursts, even alternating them within one line. In the role of Néron he cries, "At least she says nothing," cuts himself short and says "Imitate her silence," almost quietly, and in muted tones. He achieves admirable effects from these contrasts, for example, in the arrogance with which he detaches from the text Racine's innumerable exclamations of "Madame!" and uses them as foils for an anger which he shows as little as possible.

This method delights some people and infuriates others.

His silent scenes, in which Narcissus, Burrhus and Agrippina speak to him, result from a meeting of his extremes. This gives them the same intensity of contour as the gaps in my lines when I draw faces. Here also our actor's methods equal those of a poet, for both of them bring the same heraldic and geometric care to the emphasizing of space.

And this silent listening by Marais in the midst of his part acquires the power of handwriting. It forces us to follow, above his silence, the words pronounced by his partner.

Jean Marais uses empty space, which belongs to artists, and silence, which belongs to musicians. In *Les Parents Terribles* the surface of his presences is circumscribed by that of his absences. They establish its contour.

By prolonging his presence in an idealized way after his exits, and projecting it before his entrances, he helps me to put him on stage when he is off. For he must remain the center, the *idée fixe*, of this family and those who observe them. My text would not be enough to bring this out.

The excess and reserve which he sometimes mingles rather clumsily form a sublime knot at the end of the film *L'Eternel Retour*. At this point he truly incarnates the horn solo from the third act of *Tristan und Isolde* when the horn winds and unwinds, ceases to become music in order to become twilight and exquisite torture, when you imagine it is going to blend into the orchestra, yet it begins again and only blends into it after going into all the grottoes of the heart.

The scene was being filmed at the Victorine in Nice. The beauty of each take was so nearly frightening that no one dared to move or whisper, the dressers wept and the cameramen walked on tiptoe.

This atmosphere, which is rare on the set, lasted until the phrase, "I cannot keep my life any longer," which stops the camera at one of the most beautiful images to which the cinema can aspire.

Jean Marais tries to climb back up the slope of errors which leads the public to confuse a versified anecdote with a poem, and films with the use that Shakespeare and Goethe might have made of them, a use quite different from that which they made of the theater, even in *The Tempest* and *Faust Part Two*. A new kind of use, which we attempted, in opposition to custom, in *Le Sang d'un Poète* and *Orphée*, in order to place an art which lacks its Aristotle.

On the road to my country house in Seine-et-Oise, I come to the Tecalemit factory, and every time I pass it the word "Tecalemit" frightens me. It re-echoes within me like the cry of the birds which announce the white giant in the journal of Arthur Gordon Pym.

Tecalemit! Tecalemit! To whom shall I confess the almost religious fear this word provokes in me? Nobody would understand me. Tecalemit, they would reply, is a lubrication process. And I would remain alone in the world with this fateful word and the dangers that it forebodes.

The moon terrifies me. My fear of it dates from childhood and an illustration to Jules Verne which preceded those of Max Ernst. It showed a bearded man in a frock coat, holding a child by the hand. With his free hand he was pointing to the moon. Underneath you could read these words: *"The moon!" said the doctor.*

I don't know if it was the word "doctor," the cliff or the dark silhouette of the two people; the fact remains that this little phrase would throw me into a panic.

It is true, nonetheless, that I cannot see the moon that poets describe to us. Instead I see a frightening ball, a ruin with neon lighting.

I speak elsewhere of certain pompous minuets which frighten me.

In this way things affect each mind differently. They open up new vistas within it, or slide over the surface. The reader may reject this book, believing that actors are not worth examination. That Tecalemit, the moon, minuets and the case of Marais are evidence of my fantasies. But is writing not a means of confiding these fantasies to those who feel similar ones? I know that people like anecdotes and that my distaste for anecdotes is not popular. Readers will object that malevolence and falsehood are everywhere, that benevolence and truth have no value. I persist in believing that this is not the case. Too many people write to me about their disappointment at never finding any serious information about the artists they like.

And let no one accuse me of a tendency to praise, for blame is an easy way of flattering oneself with the false perspicacity one shows in it. I detest the cold water of praise withheld. It reminds me of the song *Tout Va Très Bien, Madame la Marquise*, a song which nearly became (and deservedly so) the national anthem of the French Government Information Office.

The gulf between science and belief completes our destruction. They each pull in their own direction. This creates a neutral zone where people flounder about.

I only like artists who know how to blend the material and the spiritual within their minds, and who organize a temple of Eleusis for themselves in an uncivilized era which is unmasked when its ignorance of proportion assumes the shape of furniture or buildings. In this way it solves the mystery, which is unfathomable.

Jean Marais represents for me the athlete of the inner temple. There is no Pythagoras, alas, for this emulator of Milon of Crotona, who shone in the stadium.

I salute an actor who made his profession into a religion and a science and then reconciled them in his own sphere, and to whose life we could apply the rules used for checking the Golden Number.

Giorgio de Chirico

Most of the descriptions in this book are admiring portraits of people Cocteau knew well, even if the acquaintanceship operated mainly across the footlights. The two pieces that follow, almost like two episodes in a serial story, are about the painter Giorgio de Chirico, very much a contemporary of Cocteau, since he was only one year older than the poet and all his enduring work was done between 1910 and 1925, when Cocteau was active in the world of ballet and theater, while writing poésie critique *in dramatic style. This diptych is no portrait composed in the same style as those of Edouard de Max or even Colette. There are no amusing descriptions of how Chirico wore his hair or whether the two men shared an omelette for lunch.* Le Mystère Laïc[1] *is truly an essay in indirect criticism, one of the stirring examples of* poésie critique *in Cocteau's early manner, when he had reached the second or even the third stage of* enfance terrible, *for he was over thirty at the time, writing with a kind of tense brilliance but fortunately avoiding imitations of himself. He achieves here a portrait which is as far removed from caricature as possible, in a sense "metaphysical," in harmony with the "metaphysics" of Chirico's painting. He does not set out to describe or explain Chirico or his work, but illuminates them from the periphery, using at the same time a kind of telescopic lens which penetrates even the impenetrable Chirico mannequins.*

There is more to all this than Chirico; on the peripheral line are all the familiar Cocteau ideas and accessories, from the "invisibility" of Radiguet to the "exactness" of poetry; Cocteau put

[1] First published in 1928. The text used here is that from *Poésie Critique*, Paris, 1959.

this essay together like a piece of music, going back to his central theme as a composer does, as though to prove that all his modulations and changes of rhythm are there at least partly so that we can admire the dexterity of his return. No wonder that circus acrobats made such an impression on Cocteau: he wanted to perform his numéro *too, and here we have to watch, not only read him, while looking both up and down. Either he has dispensed with the safety net or else he has invented an invisible one.*

It is fair to say that present-day readers can appreciate Cocteau's portraits without having seen or met the originals, but since the essay on Chirico is a portrait of a painter inclusive of his painting, it is as well to know something of the work; otherwise one's enjoyment of the indirect criticism remains merely technical. Only those readers who know Chirico's work well can realize the comprehensive and stimulating scope of this short piece, in which actual titles of paintings are not mentioned. The titles that occur are in fact those of Cocteau's own works or those of his friends and heroes. There is no better proof that Benedetto Croce was right in condemning the "impersonality" of art criticism: obviously it is the intensely personal approach that remains in the mind.

Driven out of my house by dust, memories, photographs, letters and fetishes of all kinds I shall probably no longer live anywhere. I would like to put these notes and my study on Picasso on the chimney piece *in that place.*

I reserve the right to live and make friends (more difficult than making love) in front of these family portraits who deserve my gratitude and respect.

Chirico's family on his father's side: uncle and aunt mad. His uncle used to push a chair along as he walked to stop himself from falling over a precipice. His aunt Olympia would undo her hair, kneel down in front of a sofa and rub her head on it until she went bald. Such antecedents contribute to remove any picturesque character from Chirico's work.

Chirico's brother Savinio[2] was a musician and a poet. He be-

[2] Andrea de Chirico, three years younger, was a composer and a

gan to paint. A naïve collector wondered which of the two brothers took his inspiration from the other and why they influenced each other. In fact they authenticated each other. Savinio proved that family feeling and childhood memories motivated Chirico. They were two brothers of Italian origin, brought up in Greece, supervised from an Acropolis by their mother, wearing full evening dress, seated on a ballroom chair, with a bouquet of roses in her hand.

A man who falls out of a window is a man who grows smaller and suddenly stops growing smaller, posing like a mannequin. A man who moves away is a man who falls gently and instead of being crushed to death evaporates like a cloud. All Chirico's perspectives are falls.

Photographing a house does not give the same effect as filming it. Even when nothing moves, the cinema still registers something else. There is nothing more intriguing than a photograph in the middle of a film. It should be used to catch characters under the influence of fear.[3]

Among other paintings Chirico's paintings look as though they have been turned into statues like this, they have the antique calm of accidents which have just taken place and reveal speed surprised by immobility without having had time to make preparations.

The horror caused by an accident encountered on our way is due to the fact that it consists of motionless speed, a cry turned into silence (and not silence after a cry). The dead can be recognized immediately because of their grotesque attitudes which cause no wish to laugh. A picture by Chirico perpetuates the rapid passage from one state to another. The strange position of all kinds of objects does not make us laugh; the human soul is never mistaken about the nature of this group of dusty mannequins, even if we do not look at them.

prolific writer. One of his plays, *Les Chants de la Mi-mort*, was published by Apollinaire in his Soirées de Paris in 1914. There was clearly some interaction between the work of the two brothers. Andrea, who wrote under the name of Alberto Savinio, died in 1953.

[3] I did it in *Le Sang d'un Poète*. (Author's note.)

In the wings of the Renaissance, orthopedics and anatomy were only waiting for a sign from Chirico to come on stage.

The life of a pure man should not consist of any act which could easily become legal before the courts, and the courts can never equal the effort of a pure man. A pure man ceases to be so as soon as he accepts a favorable situation and takes advantage of anything.

I do not see a single motive in the painter with whom I am concerned which could look innocent in the eyes of judges, plead his cause for him and save his skin. There was nobody at the scene of the crime. The smallest biscuit could give evidence against him.

Poetry is exactness, figures. But people find inexactness poetic and romantic. The crowd adore inexactness which seems true. I wonder if the blackmail-type newspapers relate inexact things because they learn them at fourth hand or whether they falsify truth through a deep understanding of public taste.

The public perceives a reality behind the apparent unreality of a Chirico painting; *they are not taken in.*

To judge *Le Rappel à l'Ordre*[4] from the aesthetic point of view is to confuse tools with *objets d'art.*

I am not interested in establishing whether Chirico paints better or worse, whether he repeats himself or invents something new. If I did this I would be assuming an aesthetic point of view. Chirico interests me from the ethical point of view. He proves to me the existence of a truth of the soul, since he never has anything picturesque along with all the elements which serve him.

A great artist is inhuman, vegetable and bestial. If he tries to talk, his efforts overwhelm us. The Stravinsky of *Le Sacre* is a tree growing. The Stravinsky of *L'Histoire du Soldat,* the *Sérénade* and *Oedipus Rex* is the tree trying to talk and succeeding.[5]

---

[4] An important collection of Cocteau's *poésie critique,* published in 1926, including essays written since 1918, such as *Le Coq et l'Harlequin* and *Le Secret Professionel.*

[5] *Le Sacre du Printemps* was the Nijinsky ballet of 1913. *The*

Chirico talks all the time. He often talks through a ventriloquist. Sometimes he talks on his own: then he has a relapse. There is nothing more moving than an animal trying to rediscover the secret of human speech which it had found once and then lost.

Chirico removes his orthopedic corset and no longer hides behind the Italian professionalism of *trompe-l'oeil*.

Audacity develops alongside the audacious. A man who prolongs an old audacity is found to be audacious. Everyone believed themselves to be superior from 1920 to 1927 because the obscure type of art was entering its rococo period.

A man like Picasso used to swallow swords, which left him with a bitter taste in his mouth. A man like Miró[6] sucks pieces of barley sugar until they are pointed. The point gets sharper and sharper but the barley sugar gets shorter and shorter.

Miró is saved by his living line. He only has to draw a cross in order to crucify.

Miró's influence on the first strip cartoons: *Felix the Cat.*

I believe that art reflects morality and that one cannot renew oneself without leading a dangerous life and causing gossip. That is the only wall between Maritain[7] and myself. In essence he thinks that art is a dangerous game, a caricature of creation, a trap, while morality is stable, having been established once and for all.

This is true if he looks back over that long reign of aestheti-

Soldier's Tale, as *L'Histoire du Soldat* is called in English, is a moving setting of a "morality" by the Swiss writer C. F. Ramuz and was first performed in Lausanne in 1919. For the secular oratorio *Oedipus Rex* (1928) Cocteau had written (with Jean Daniélou) a scenario in Latin. The work has had an enduring success.

[6] The Spanish painter Joán Miró, b. 1893.

[7] The great Catholic thinker Jacques Maritain had a distinct influence on Cocteau and on many others of his generation. Maritain and Cocteau exchanged open letters in 1925 and 1926, discussing questions of faith, ethics, the principles of art, etc.

cism and cruelty when the heart seemed ridiculous. But its ice is now beginning to melt. Everything changes. The plastic code is followed by a moral type of plasticity which is not judged with the intelligence. The new criticism will demand the use of the heart, that is to say, it will become a task which is less easy and will finally disappear. One of Chirico's merits is that in the midst of the plastic period he has relied more on morality than on visual problems, which are fated to end in preciousness.

It is not a question of looking without understanding and enjoying gratuitously a decorative charm. It is a question of paying dearly and understanding with a special sense: the sense of the marvelous.

People demand to have poetry explained to them. They are unaware that poetry is a closed world to which very few are admitted and sometimes nobody at all.

The things imagined by Chirico are shown full face. They follow us everywhere like those portraits in which the eyes are ingeniously painted in the middle. It should be noticed in literature that Stendhal, among others, handles his characters in this way. As a result readers of the most widely different types recognize themselves in Julien Sorel and say to themselves at every line in *The Red and the Black*: "That's me." A man like Dostoevski paints a three-quarter view, all mixed up.

We admire the interplay of shadow and perspectives. We do not feel put out by one eye. (No doubt if I were Russian I would write the contrary.)

"No one can be a poet without wings, but we must still take care that Pegasus does not get lost on the solitary heights where he would be his only spectator." (*Voyage de Sparte*.)

How prudent of Barrès![8] There is a way, however: Why does the hero, the giver of advice, not mount the horse? Unfortunately, solitude does not last long. Transport is organized

[8] The novelist and essayist who lived from 1862 to 1923. Two of his best-known works are *La Colline Inspirée* and *Les Déracinés*, the latter forming the first part of a trilogy. Cocteau's *Visites à Barrès* was included in *Le Rappel à l'Ordre* (1926).

quickly and luxury hotels also, but that is not the beginning. Chirico! Picasso! The horse who least suspected he would become a spectacle.

For this reason one keeps solitude even after people have arrived. Picasso keeps it because he is full, Chirico because he is empty. These two obstacles prevent the public from coming in.

It happens also that professionalism gives works a finished aspect, making them look fastened up and firmly locked, preventing sensitive people from coming in and playing a part.

Matisse, in whom professionalism is a form of genius, looks therefore as though he has none. That is why this great painter is so pleasing. The collector imagines that he can finish the painting and that it demands his collaboration. Picasso and Chirico chill the public. One might say that they see written on Picasso's still-life paintings: *please keep out*, and on Chirico's streets: *no entry*. But this prohibition does not run the risk of disappearing down the slope which I have mentioned, since our painters have taken care not to give their perfection the shape of a ball.

Something permitted cannot be pure.

Many of Chirico's paintings are blind, but none of them are deaf. We are assured that deaf people are more unhappy than blind ones. However, the deaf man belongs to comedy and the blind one to tragedy.

Chirico is a poet. He does not upset me. It appears that I have greatly upset certain artists because of an interview. It was stated in it that I do sculpture. In fact I don't. I try rather to draw in space with the snow-white wire of pipe cleaners.[9] But if I wanted to do sculpture I would. Sometimes ink revolts me. Poetry expresses itself in whichever way it can. I do not restrict it in any way. I am free. I have made a film;[10] in this period without countries I have leaped over the wall of languages. I am not a

---

[9] He did in fact create a kind of sculpture with pipe cleaners. There is a famous photograph by Man Ray which shows him at work, the shadows of the wire imparting a *craquelure* effect to his face.

[10] *Le Sang d'un Poète.*

poet with aims. I do not seek places, rewards or admiration. Admiration leaves me cold. My work demands love and I receive it. As Antigone[11] said, nothing else matters to me. If I upset people, displease or disturb them, then that is too bad. I detest people who go around in circles. I am a spoilsport.

The objects in a Chirico painting have not made appointments with each other.

Before operating on her, Chirico has given Venus chloroform.

People are always talking about religious art. Art *is* religious. A true crucifixion results from Picasso's anger against painting. Works made of nails, fabric, torn-up scraps, wood, blood, bile.

Chirico never gets angry. The calmness of his work is that of archers in primitive paintings who attend an execution and look outside the picture.

People believe that realists are madmen who fill the museums. A museum is a morgue. The only chance of feeling any emotion is to recognize a friend there. A friend behind the corpse. A beautiful picture is a proof of dead activity. In these exhausting races through rooms which smell of death, we only become aware of our legs again in front of outstanding works.

What a mistake to think that masterpieces are simple! We are comforted by a Poussin, a Claude, a Corot, or an Ingres, we wonder by what miracle these jokers are preserved. No doubt a kind of false resemblance with reality deceives everyone, just as Radiguet deceived the world because his genius looked like talent. Otherwise I demand a breathtaking likeness. Go and look again at the masks of Antinoüs in the Musée Guimet. They are not impassioned. This is what saves them from being luxuries and allows them to live in semi-darkness, on plinths of red unreal plush which is ragged, faded and silvered over with white dust.

[11] Cocteau's adaptation in contemporary prose of Sophocles' tragedy, produced by Charles Dullin at the Atelier during the winter of 1922–23. Dullin himself played Créon and Cocteau the Chorus. *Décor* by Picasso, costumes by Chanel. Cocteau has said that it was an attempt to photograph Greece from an airplane.

Picasso deceives the mind. I mean that in order to trick our birds he invented worthwhile grapes. Chirico uses *trompe-l'oeil* as a criminal reassures his victim: "Don't be afraid. You see, there's a bell, the window isn't a false one, the door's open, you've only to call out. . . ."

Realism consists in copying exactly the objects in a world belonging to the artist and without the slightest connection with what is usually regarded as reality.

At the Luxembourg, once one has paid homage to Renoir and Manet, one can only look without disgust, one mediocrity in return for another, at well-painted pictures; for example, *Professor X . . . Performing an Operation, Surrounded by His Students.* The paintings by the artists who laughed at these well-painted pictures have become ridiculous.

Chirico the careful painter. He borrows from dreams this exactness of inexactness, this use of the true to plead the cause of the false. He carefully transports the reality of his mind onto his canvas as the primitives copied miracles. Since he does not have to transmit his faith, he transmits his confidence.

One day our age will be called the age of mystery. People paint mystery as they used to paint the circus. Chirico is a painter of mystery. Picasso is a mysterious painter. His mystery comes from the fact that he is a great painter and that all greatness is mysterious. The mystery of elegance: *Adolphe, La Princesse de Clèves,* La Fontaine's Fables, *Le Bal du Comte d'Orgel,* as mysterious as *The Idiot, Une Saison en Enfer, Les Chants de Maldoror.*[12]

Elegance, much more so than obscurity, makes a work invisible. Picasso is elegance itself. This ensures him of invisibility. For the first time the artist placed the mind, and not the mirror, not even a deforming mirror, in front of the object. Picasso's work is disguised, masked, therefore mysterious. He intrigues. But Chirico is a painter of mystery. For he substitutes the portraits

[12] The theme that invisibility is tantamount to elegance recurs continually in Cocteau's work. He has often quoted Beau Brummel's remark to George IV: "I could not have been elegant the other night because you noticed me."

of miracles, with which the primitives surprise us, for miracles which are his alone.

Incredulity, of which the first stage is platitude, soon forces the artist to use an inventive lyricism to replace the mysticism of the religious painters who *copied miracles*. We should not confuse a martyr carrying his own head and a mannequin who walks only through the painter's will power. In fact Chirico is a religious painter. A religious painter without faith. A painter of lay mystery. He needs miracles. His realism prevents him from painting miracles to which he would add no faith. He has to produce some, therefore, by uprooting objects and persons.

True realism consists in revealing astonishing things which habit conceals beneath a dust-sheet and prevents us from seeing. Our name no longer has a human shape. We do not hear it. A postman can wake us by calling it out in a hotel corridor, a cashier asks us for it, schoolboys who laugh at it in the classroom pull off the dust-sheet and suddenly reveal this name which is detached from us, solitary and strange like an unknown object. A Louis XVI armchair strikes us when we see it in front of the antique shop, chained to the pavement. What an odd sort of dog! It's a Louis XVI armchair. In a drawing-room nobody would have noticed it.

Chirico shows us reality by uprooting it. He is an un-landscape painter. The remarkable circumstances in which he places a building, an egg, a rubber glove or a plaster head remove the dust-sheet of habit and make them fall out of the sky as an aeronaut falls among savages, endowing them with the importance of divinity.

The appropriateness of relationships, even the oddest of them, is totally different from decorative oddness. Everything which is beautiful is true, and its reality gives away the existence of another world. We become aware of this truth merely through the feeling that it exists, the feeling of moral comfort. It usually happens that this truth corresponds one day to something familiar in our world and so loses all its marvelous quality. I'm not talking about symbols. Simple minds bring them into everything they don't understand; it is their way of reassuring themselves.

I repeat, since concerts have been broadcast from the Eiffel Tower, the cyclist scene in *Les Mariés de la Tour Eiffel*[13] has taken on a clever, that is to say, a vulgar meaning.

Allegory, the opposite of symbol.

This celestial truth, which contains no symbols, gives a prophetic tone to certain works. For example, when Apollinaire was wounded, Chirico painted the poet's wound on his forehead in advance, and one day when I was with Dullin,[14] draping the white fabric used in the prologue to *Antigone* around a dressmaker's dummy, by a table covered with an architect's instruments, I suddenly found myself face to face with a picture by Chirico.

Apart from a certain air of solemnity Chirico's paintings borrow nothing from dreams. His paintings seem rather as though they are sleeping and dreaming of nothing. I like it when a young painter (Christian Bérard) paints a man asleep instead of following the fashion and painting a dream. The man who sleeps and does not dream, or dreams too deeply to remember his dreams, moves me greatly. Dreams are the literature of sleep. Even the strangest ones compose with memories. The best part of a dream evaporates in the morning. There remains only the impression of a volume, the ghost of an incident, the memory of a memory, the shadow of a shadow. This uneasiness has no more value than luncheon-table drawings made by several people on a piece of folded paper. When we wake up we watch our dreams like a spectator listening to a play in a foreign language.

Before a dream can keep its strength and live like seaweed in the sea we need a machine to register it during sleep.

When we describe our dreams we make the same mistake which in 1916 consisted of describing machines. Take an example from machines and dreams. Compose a poem with the mechanism

[13] Described as an "entertainment," first produced by Les Ballets Suédois in Paris, 1921, and published two years later. An amusing, ironic work with music, some of it *pastiche*, by *Les Six*, regarded by some as Cocteau's first truly original creation and recently translated into English for use in schools: presumably therefore a classic of the avant-garde.

[14] See p. 107, note 11.

of dream. A face which becomes another face. A word which changes meaning on the way. See and sea.

Max Jacob's[15] puns are musical. Those of Marcel Duchamp[16] scorn the intellect. I have had too many reproaches about the puns in *Opéra*[17] for me not to explain myself in a few lines. *L'ami Zamore de Madame du Barry* is a fact. *La Mise à Mort de Madame du Barry* is an oracle. I have tried to rejuvenate the tradition of the Greek pun. Metaphors are badly finished puns. I pull the knot tight until the finger no longer feels anything on the cord.

It will soon be seen that my puns were not the wit but the heart of my book.

When one invents something it is pleasing to learn that the same anxieties motivated the work of artists one did not know. Base minds regard these coincidences as thefts and complain. A lofty mind regards them as the proof of necessity. When I thought of rejuvenating Greece, operating on this old singer and giving her a new skin (the work on *Antigone* and *Oedipus Rex*), I did not know that Chirico was going to place these huge figures in a white mist beside the sea, their egg-shaped heads wrapped in quantities of gossamer threads, their open chests displaying a monumental heart.

We saw them later at the Rosenberg Gallery. For want of something better, I would have liked to hang these trophies, boxes and scaffolding of entrails round Antigone's neck. The grateful city spits on Creon.

[15] The Cubist poet who lived from 1876 to 1944. Puns were a feature of his poetry, his best-known collection being the prose poems *Le Cornet à dés* (1918).

[16] b. 1887, he was associated with Dada and Surrealism, later going to the U.S.A. where he concentrated on "anti-art."

[17] One of Cocteau's most important collections of poems (1927). From time to time puns are declared to be unfashionable or a sign of bad taste, but many writers, notably Shakespeare, have been unable to resist them. Cocteau uses them as part of his explorations into the extreme potentialities of language. The two phrases quoted here in French sound identical when spoken.

My Contemporaries

A rubber glove hanging beside a plaster head, a deserted street, an egg placed in a destructive solitude, lighting that belongs to an eclipse and an outbreak of plague: it is normal for all this to lead our painter to the drama of Aeschylus or Sophocles and conjure up these tragic actors side by side, with their chests opening on the tangled constructions of insects.

Chirico, who was born in Greece, no longer needs to paint Pegasus. The color, eyes and mouth of a horse by the sea give it the importance of myth. I think of the film *Ben Hur* which attracted us so much because of four white horses; they were filmed as they raced, from a vehicle following them at the same speed, and look like a solid row of disheveled profiles, sculptured out of marble wind.

Is there anything more realistic than painting the thing imagined in the room where one imagines it? A steamboat surrounded with spray, a locomotive coming in through the door, a clump of trees on the floor.

When Chirico places a Greek temple and a piece of landscape on the table we cannot tell if the temple is small or the table large. The temple is not a toy, one of those strip cartoons including both caricature and film, but truly petrified imagination, taken to extremes and brought into the world alive and allowing no comparison between the scale of the temple and the table which live together. The astonishing thing is that the painter's execution emphasizes no difference between the room and the imagination. The truth of what he expresses becomes obvious and prevents us from regarding the temple as a model or the table as an outsize piece of furniture.

If you close your eyes in a room and recall a memory located in the same room, it is rare for one not to represent the room with the memory in another place, outside the room where one remembers it.

We would like Chirico to paint the two rooms one inside the other.

The origin of furnished landscapes must be some American comic film. Perhaps the one in which creditors remove a house piece by piece from around the owners while they are having lunch.

The earth furnishes.

We live in a world where everything should be capable of explanation, where the court asks questions and where the badly organized police force observe family secrets from outside. With Giorgio de Chirico the walls, arcades, shadows, equestrian statues and vegetables are suspect.

I imagine the police raiding one of his canvases as they raid a poet's room. It is better to keep quiet and let them cut off your head. In my room the smallest object gives evidence against me.

There is no serious art without puns and riddles. That is to say, there is only serious art. Through the naïveté of Freud we can sense the greatness of Leonardo who flies in a dream with Uccello. Whenever Freud deplores his childish behavior Leonardo da Vinci flies.

Every masterpiece is made up of concealed admissions, calculations, lofty puns and strange riddles. The world of officialdom would collapse if they discovered what was concealed by Leonardo or Watteau, to mention only two of the well-known secretive people. It is through the things which Freud regards as childish that an artist tells his own story without opening his mouth, dominates art and endures.

Chirico, or the scene of the crime.

The man of genius is the man capable of anything. Sometimes the question is raised in brutal fashion: could masterpieces be *alibis?*

Chirico is also the time of the train.

Death is the only piece which moves freely and in any direction on Chirico's chessboard.

Four years between Le Mystère Laïc *and* Les Beaux Arts Considérés Comme un Assassinat *and twenty-six years before both pieces were revised and extracted for the 1959 two-volume edition of the* Poésie Critique, Chirico *had continued to paint in a manner that most people actively disliked, for it did not seem to follow the rules of imaginative logic; why did the man who painted the silent streets, the mannequins, plaster heads and artichokes seem to go backwards instead of forwards? But who shall decide, in an absolute sense, which direction is which? An artist does what he wants to do. Only in moods of numbness does one want to know why it all happened. If we read Cocteau to find the answer, we will find only questions, apart from one private expression of dogma: in friendship he remained true to himself in befriending Chirico the whole man, the whole painter. Even if he accepts him here more indirectly than ever through the French classical dramatists, Paolo di Dono, Leonardo da Vinci, puns in prose and verse, the acceptance of the painter-poet by the poet-critic is total.*

Which is presumably why there is no reference to either of these pieces in James Thrall Soby's book on Chirico published by the Museum of Modern Art, a useful and totally prosaic work in which acceptance and appreciation remain limited.

I am alone in a world other
than myself.

Chirico is a poet who expresses himself on canvas, thanks to the Italian professionalism of *trompe-l'oeil*. His inventions are a poet's inventions. I think he would only lose if he attempted painter's inventions. When he writes, he will always win.

Never, throughout these notes, must literary painting, which is a real scourge, be confused with the type of painting now concerning us because it is painted by poets. Picasso is a painter whose pictures are poems. Chirico is a poet whose poems are pictures. It is from this point of view that they differ, resemble each other and concern us. Painting possesses its art critics and specialists. A poet looks at it; it does not look at him.

The reason I insist is in order to emphasize how mistaken it is to confuse Chirico with a literary painter. Eccentric, if you wish, but literary, no. A poet who paints, yes. Picasso is a painter who appears to write. Chirico, a poet who seems to paint.

In 1930, Chirico's book, *Hebdoméros,*[18] which had not appeared when I published *Le Mystère Laïc* for the first time, supplies the proof that Chirico's aesthetic is an ethic. I knew this very well. (What is done and what is not done, what is eaten and what is not eaten, what is clean and what is unclean, as in the Bible.)

Baudelaire and Nietzsche were concerned with hygiene.

Masterpieces of painting are objects charged with a fluid which cannot be obtained or preserved without blood, and which over the centuries acquire a hypnotic power.

When you pose for a picture, observe that the painter looks like an assassin. By accident you are in a way his accomplice.

The man who creates kills in savage fashion anything which disturbs a supreme reflex of the instinct of preservation.

This produces vehicles. After his death these vehicles continue by machine and remain capable of killing quite a lot of people. When the vehicles stop, they stop in the tragic attitude of something which has died in action, and it is this desperate attitude, this desperate anxiety to survive, to continue, to puncture time and overcome inertia, which makes certain old pictures moving. What voices, what looks these museum pictures find to prevent us from going past, to shout out "Stop!" to the tourist in order to overcome his fatigue. Through the dusty golden layer of patina and the ingeniousness of the sign of intelligence fixed by the painter in order to intrigue us and rally us from a great distance, a whole quantity of fluid spurts over us.

In museums it is the eccentric works in particular which demand our attention. By eccentric I mean those where the ingredients of immortality seem to come not so much from choice as from constraint. The sign ceases then to be any desperate

---

[18] Chirico wrote a great deal, from prose poems to studies of individual artists and articles on various aspects of art. This was his only novel, first published in French (1929 seems the correct date) and not translated into Italian until 1942.

appeal, merely any eccentric gesture, and becomes one of those indications of the enigma where the painter's life hides within the shelter of art.

Once this deceptive part has been played the masterpiece no longer counts. It returns to the crowd of masqueraders. It has introduced Romeo to Juliet, Tristan to Iseult.

Until a work of art becomes an object capable of casting a spell, it counts little.

The casting of spells demands a care and patience which the man who creates would not know how to extract from his work. This is why his hates and loves go into his work and his work casts a spell.

Any work which is not a voluntary or involuntary vehicle for confession is a luxury. Now luxury is not merely immoral, it is boring. It is the fatigue of this boredom on its shoulders which exposes luxury in art.

There is nothing more comical than plagiarist painters who are naïvely compromised by confessions they repeat without knowing it, like so many decorative themes.

The eccentricities of Cézanne when he is most painter-like are the eccentricities of an intellectual.

The eccentricities of Renoir, especially when he became old, remain the eccentricities of a painter.

Sexual vice reflects one of the most intriguing forms of aesthetics.

It is not from taste, as a collector might group furniture and fabrics, that this septuagenarian arranges the smallest details of the scenario without which he cannot satisfy his senses when daylight comes. If he disguises himself as a Louis XV soubrette, if he wears chains and submits to the insults of a telegraphist, and finally opens an obscene telegram signed by his daughter, this occurs after researches and obscure preparations which leave him no choice and end in a masquerade where his senses desperately construct an equivalent, more baroque, but in fact hardly less individual than any other, for beauty.

In order to obtain his beauty Chirico had to submit to a setting, a collaboration by accessories which can offer a spectacle of diversity or liberty but deceive no one about the drama of the adventure. And, just as the septuagenarian's scenario can frighten or amuse us, while he draws his only pleasure from it, it is probable that Chirico expected some result from his pictures that we cannot conceive, one which had not the slightest connection with our admiration and surprise.

The man who conceals a single sexual vice will not know the vague uneasiness of a body struggling with the multiple appearances of beauty. Inevitable art does not disturb the painter; it disturbs the spectators. The liberty of the inevitable painter consists in varying the aspect of his prison.

Chirico renounces the exploitation of something inevitable. It was to be feared that his brickworks manufactured phantoms. But after the brush, his fluid wanted to emerge through his pen and leave the painter free to abandon himself to the innocent games which never compromise anyone except ourselves.

The professional preoccupation of art critics distracts them from the very object of their study. The principal question was (and remains) to know why Giorgio de Chirico played chess, the amount of the stakes and the strength and personality of the adversary.

A woman's glove, a red glove made of dog skin, it is said, moved the pieces against the painter on the chessboard in this formidable game.

A man's works express his life (his vices, eccentricities and morals). It would be impossible to write a life of Picasso, for this painter's monstrous beauty resides in the fact that his life is his work. He works as others live. And he lives as others sleep. His mania is a mania for painting. This is why his work is a drama. For Picasso, ripping a canvas can assume the importance of a murder, and have results as serious as they were invisible or illegal. With him, prison would be just another painting.

Hell, just another painting.

My Contemporaries

A great painter proves his presence only by a single cry: "I am here." It is Uccello's horse which raises both legs on the same side, which shocks Vasari greatly. It is the shadow on the sunny side in the Rubens[19] which Goethe shows to Eckermann. It is the painter's artichoke in a city reserved exclusively for statues.

A pure man should be free and suspect. A poet will never be light enough in style, nor heavy enough. In the long run everything subsides and unloosens. The main thing is to be in shelter (dead) at the moment of unloosening.

Baudelaire did not pull things tight enough; he came undone too quickly. Is one of our puns not exactly like a spiritual knot? A jewel of invisibility.

Stendhal's system of invisibility was one of extreme lightness. He had subsided, just as objects subside in a case during a journey. He acquired his volume when he was no longer there to suffer from it. Moreover, there has never been room for a man and his work together. You cannot be and have been. You must enjoy being alive or being dead. Fame is subject to the laws of perspective. You can't cheat, except through *trompe-l'oeil*.

Celebrity: I think of a bust with legs for running everywhere.

In short, one must be invisible until further orders. Invisible, that is to say, fast enough, or slow enough, or loose enough, or tight enough to be disapproved of by one's contemporaries, in the most superficial sense and in the most serious sense of the term. That is style, for, as you know, no decorative style ever exists. Style is the soul, and unfortunately with us the soul affects the shape of the body.

The chimneys of Chirico's factories, where his emptiness and silence are manufactured.

All in all, I think that one of the greatest expressions of nobility in Chirico's work is the atmosphere of his towns. There reigns there, you might say, a counterpart of popular celebrations, patriotic rejoicing and funerals of great leaders. It is not that trophies are lacking, nor heroism. The flags are hung out upside

[19] I have made the mistake on several occasions of attributing this engraving to Rembrandt. (Author's note.)

down, and you can enjoy here that peace of nocturnal towns where moonlight and emptiness set the scene, where a few rare civilians meditate rapid and inglorious crimes. Green statues are set up there, as though they had grown up through the asphalt, in naïve and vegetable fashion—Baudelaire, Sade, Colonel Picquart, Raymond Roussel[20]—and were it not for the narrowness of a painter's canvas, one would like to read the names of the streets and the squares, which do not change with the fate of arms.

Chirico's towns conjure up the reverse of the celebrations or funerals which deck our towns with flags. Their character is essentially anti-national.

Silence, led by music, marches through Chirico's streets.

During entire nights my eye has surveyed these docks, this labyrinth of disturbing warehouses where the human figure has no value, where man finds no place.

The eloquent silence of Chirico, this orator who reflects.

The silence of Chirico. The silence of the sale-room. There is also the silence of the green tables at Monte Carlo with those old English goddesses, always standing, ancient youthfulness, gentle columns wearing hats trimmed with daylight, decorated with real birds who walk around the brims, behind the eggs they have laid.
Religiously alike, daughters of the golden numbers, fortified with the laws of heaven, the casino supports them; and to be truthful, these gentle columns support the casino, remaining its wandering caryatids.

Chirico, monster of naïveté. He wants to please. If he wants to cause fear, he does so. It was wonderful to see him, at the *Ballets Russes*, bowing, as though he was drunk, after his panto-mime, bowing, bowing, catching his foot, jostling the people in the wings, emerging suddenly from the deathly silence of private views into a din of applause, like the bull from the darkness of the *toril*.

[20] See p. 59.

Chirico's personality, his scope. His horse-like head, his plaster mask with gold teeth, his rough accent, his real presence and his painted or written presence, all this amounts to a large format which deflates everything one can put forward against him as better painted, more haunted, more upright, more serious, more courageous, and turns an attitude which annoys his former followers, a new attitude he has taken up, into something outside taste, something singular and disturbing for the same reason, in a sphere which after all is less attractive than his early pictures.

Paris, a doomed city, a city of grown-ups. There are poets *and* grown-ups. How did the grown-ups, Voltaire, Diderot and Grimm, fail to get the better of Jean-Jacques, who was childish? I am speaking of the Jean-Jacques of the Héron fountain. He finds himself, until the end, the Rousseau who wears Persian dress on the excuse of caution, the Rousseau who composes an eclogue with the police on his heels.[21]

Doomed cities. Cities which have lost childhood: Paris, city of grown-ups. Grown-ups lock children in a dark room. The Parisians put poets in prison and kill them.

A poet's defects allow him to take root in the attention paid to him, and to wait until respect in the end imposes the rest.

A poet is only seen through his defects. One can hardly imagine a work almost totally pure, that is, almost completely invisible like *Les Tragédiens* by Desbordes.[22]

The misapprehension which makes the reader believe that he is seeing *Les Enfants Terribles*[23] ceases when the work takes off towards the end and becomes quite pure. He says then that I am letting go.

[21] For more details, see Cocteau's study of Rousseau which was dictated in 1939.

[22] Jean Desbordes was deeply influenced by *Le Grand Ecart* and by Cocteau himself. He wrote *J'Adore*, admiringly prefaced by Cocteau; a novel, *Les Tragédiens* (1930); and *Le Vrai Visage du Marquis de Sade*, a study of distinct value. He was later killed by the Gestapo.

[23] Cocteau's novel of 1929, filmed in 1950.

Baudelaire: his gifts as a painter are defects in his writing, and make it visible. Chirico: his gifts as a *littérateur* are defects in his painting, and make it visible.

Two ways of being invisible: Radiguet's style is like Beau Brummel's dress—no mannerism, no patina, but the good fortune of making novelty look like something we have seen before. He shades in the line. Desbordes leaves it raw. Radiguet remains invisible because we think we are seeing something else, Desbordes because we don't.

"*Hebdoméros?* Don't know it," a remark one might hear spoken in all sincerity by countless disciples. For this strange man, whose silence exerts such fascination that a whole generation of youth was influenced by it without even being aware of the fact, seems to walk among the dancers, with his arms folded, wearing Rocambole's fancy dress.

Chirico's paintings, even when framed, look as though they have no frames, or at least remain in the memory as having no frames. This is due to natural limits, to the fact that the painter was decorating the four walls of his prison.[24]

Giorgio de Chirico and Salvador Dali relieve themselves. Painters who relieve themselves.

One has only to look at a painting by Dali to be sure that he possesses an inevitable point of view on all things, that he inhabits a world which he dominates. He is the typical poet-painter with an ethic. He would be incapable of undertaking the slightest exchange with the outside. His money is only current in his own country, which limits exchange. He can only pay in medals, cameos or enamels.[25]

Salvador Dali has no choice; he lives in a closed world.

Bérard has the choice; he possesses the astonishing superiority of a weakness. He is a world open to assassins and ghosts.

[24] Compare Cocteau's use of the same image in the talk on Picasso (p. 66).

[25] Sartre regards this as counterfeit money (1958). (Author's note.)

Each of his pictures, therefore, is a victory over the intruders who disturb him and over aesthetics. Since he is free to contrive things he remains pure.

His work does not *seem* to be taking a place in the history of painting. It is unrecognizable strength, without any of its conventional attributes.

He paints the nuances of form.

The birds were so life-like. The grapes were mistaken about them.

Bérard: a certain corruption in his painting attracts the flies; he drives them off.

In order to deceive corruption, Dali paints his flies.

It can happen that certain faces by Christian Bérard dream of certain pictures by Salvador Dali.

The weakness of an artist is to start a school. If he starts a school instead of remaining alone, enigmatic and in some way inviolable, it is because his work contained an element that could move away from it. Chirico cannot start a school from a plastic point of view. His influence is of a moral order. Plastically it could only end in pastiche. The same was not true of the first Impressionists, or the Cubists.

Opéra. I found the title of my poems in Villefranche. It was an oracular book. It needed this play on words, a pedantic exactness which also evoked red and gold. A box at the opera is Jocasta's throne. The opera chandelier is Jocasta hanged.

I wonder if Chirico was not prompting me while I was at Villefranche inventing the tone of the poems which make up the *Musée Secret d'Opéra.* I thought this as I listened to myself reciting *Le Buste, Le Théâtre Grec* on a gramophone record, in a voice which was no longer mine and could have been that of a Chirico mannequin.

The moon is the sunshine of statues.

The inanimate drawings of Chirico.

It really looks as though the public regarded poetry with indulgence because they believed it was synonymous with lying. Since Baudelaire, poems have been suspect. The public fear poetry all the more as they discover that it conceals, beneath the flattering appearances of falsehood, one of the most embarrassing forms of truth.

On more points than one, Chirico resembles Racine. He accompanies his pomp, his unity of time, place, light, I would say, and death. Just as the dramatist bought recipes from La Voisin,[26] the painter seems to obtain from some Italian enchantress his fetiches and signs—fruit, vegetables, gloves, plaster casts, mannequins—emblems which he uses to make his fame triumphant.

Chirico administers poison through sending gloves, biscuits, cotton reels, vegetables and plaster masks. The painter even makes careful use of certain grooves in the flooring, certain arrangements of angles, deserted streets and bronze statues of political figures with their backs turned.

At the Comédie Française I used to enjoy going through a labyrinth of corridors, peristyles, parquet floors, storerooms full of disturbing furniture, cardboard chimney-pieces, balustrades, candelabras, painted draperies, busts. . . . "Yes," I would think, "it is with a silence resembling the word *Madame* as spoken by Racine's characters, a silence like his rhymes which are exhausted tenses of verbs, his noble ruses, that Chirico's mannequins must communicate between each other. His mannequins with his factory chimneys, his shadows carried with his statues of famous men, his cotton reels with his T-squares, his cork floats with his gloves."

All in all, Chirico also reminds me of Molière. What settings for discussions in cruel farces! I think of something wild and hard which saves Molière from French common sense, which links him with the *trompe-l'oeil* effects of moonlight. His marquis, his soubrettes, his lovers and dupes talk in the empty street where Chirico's accessories remain silent.

[26] A woman who was burned alive in 1677 for her alleged part in *l'affaire des poisons,* a plot directed against the royal family.

It is this Molière, invisible to his contemporaries—although they must have reacted to him as to water with iron properties—whose ideal settings would be those by Picasso for *Mercure*. One can imagine *Amphitryon*[27] with the prologue of this recumbent night!

How many innocent people, bewitched and moved surreptitiously, like chessmen, towards suicide, by formidable objects, pieces of furniture, walls, proportions, curves, papers, curtains, cornices, a lamp, a bed on which their eye rests each day, without even noticing them.

Unless one is a lover of modern art, a glance at the torn canvases by Chirico, piled up at the back of Paul Guillaume's[28] shop, was enough to make one thing evident: the choice of these *décors* and these objects was not of a sensuous nature, was not due to a taste for contrast or assembly. It was not a question of pleasing or displeasing. Such painting seemed to me a riddle, a kind of oracle, a charade, like a druggist's sign, a target which the marksman should hit at other periods and in other places.

How many profoundly distracted men penetrated into *trompe-l'oeil* and did not return.

The Medicis had their astronomers, their alchemists, their painters of perspective.

In Florence it is not rare to discover one or several skeletons behind a perspective, within the thickness of the demolished walls.

Peindre à la fresque. Feindre à la presque.

The Renaissance used perspective for the same purposes as they used magic and poison. This is why so many princes maintained painters and attached them to their person. The theater at Vicenza remains to us as a proof of these vast machines which often cost a fortune and caused death without leaving any trace.

How many unfortunate people, attracted by some rendezvous, entered the labyrinth of this formidable masterpiece, growing

[27] Molière's comedy, first produced in 1668.
[28] The famous art dealer.

smaller, disappearing as you watched, not even realizing the kind of trap whose victims they were.

Leonardo-wise

In order to catch the bear, build a courtyard measuring seven feet by eight. Have it painted black, have a canvas stretched over it. After it has been raining, place against one of the walls a young man and a young woman embracing, their hair hanging loose. Place on the young woman's face a feeling of distress which can be read in the curve of the eyelids and the mouth, and on the young man's face a feeling of scorn, and cold beauty. The bear will come in; at first he will start to walk towards the two people, but he will stop, growl, and roll amiably on the tiles of your courtyard.

Cygnet Ring

Here are the rules to bring a poem success:
Sometimes an eagle will wear a swan's dress;
Find a black swan, take him by surprise
Cracking the egg from which a son-hero flies,
Fraternal, double, painted by some maniac,
Young swan-sign promised to the fire of the Zodiac.

Paolo di Dono had been living for two months in a little cell on the ground floor of a modest house. The cell was let to him, and his food was placed on the window-sill. His friends would say in ironic fashion: "Paolo has got one of those surprises in store for us, the ones that concern only himself, in which his art goes to extremes."

One day, in the evening, he opened the window and called a little boy who was playing. He had just finished a *trompe-l'oeil* painting; it showed a cloister, with a wall on the left and arches on the right.

The boy went in and looked, surprised at seeing this cloister whose existence he did not suspect. Paolo was holding a ball of thread like those used for flying kites. "You are going to take this thread," he told the boy, "and run as fast as you can to the end of this cloister, turn to the right and come back to where you started from. Don't let go of the thread, I will unravel it."

The boy, excited by the game, rushed into the wall, penetrating *purely and simply* into the lie. "Stop!" cried the cruel bird, as the victim of his experiment reached the corner of the arcades. The runner stopped and lost his balance, becoming immobilized in one of those violent attitudes in which photographers petrify life.

Paolo, his heart beating, approached, found that the image of the boy was flat, retouched anything that might have allowed him to be identified and make him suspect as a result. Then he cut off the thread coming out of the wall flat against the surface of the fresco. The thread stretched out tightly in the picture upset his perspectives. He scratched it out and painted it over.

The next day he invited his incredulous friends in a group. "Yes," Francesco said to him, "this *trompe-l'oeil* is first class, apart from that boy who is turning around. He looks as though he has been taken in through some error in your calculations, and his expression prevents anyone being taken in by the rest."

Fold a sheet of paper like a fan; press the folds together, pierce the entire thickness with a pin. Remove the pin, unfold the paper, flatten it until the folds disappear, and ask some countryman if it is possible for all these spaced out holes to come from one single pin prick.

The theatrical cities of Italy possess no theaters, apart from the opera, for lack of an audience. Plays are performed in the street.

Chirico, the typical Italian man of the theater, inhibited by *bel canto*, expresses himself elsewhere: in Paris, in Greek, on canvas, just as gangsters, all of them Italian, express in America the Italy of Machiavelli, the Renaissance, blood, assassinations, coats of mail, effeminate killers, poisons, acts of daring and trickery.

I had just written to Chirico to ask him the title of a picture I possess, and he had just replied: "*Good Friday*, if you like, but these impressive titles are the work of poets more royalist than the King," when I realized that it was the day before Good

Friday. That very evening, alone in my room, I was convinced that the picture was active, that something abnormal was happening in this picture which still disturbs me; in fact, there was a celebration going on. If you prefer, those infinitely flat people of whom Poincaré speaks were moving about between the pilasters.

I have just emerged, terribly upset, from the account by Michel Vieuchange, chewed up, crushed and spewed out again by the Rio del Oro and Smara, the ghost town. What an unforgettable photograph of the return, following that of the departure. What prison photograph, what portrait of a dead poet can match it? A look which looks at us *and which sees the town*. With the brief spectacle of a dead town, a strong young man exchanges his life. Could he pay more dearly for a caprice, or rather, an obsession?

The look on someone's face is never spoken of enough. The look of a portrait reflects the anxieties of its period. It burns with a dark or chilling fire. It reflects so much and so well that already in Cézanne an iridescent speck forms on the eye, gazing at the orbit and the iris rather than inner problems. Later, the speck grows until the time of Picasso, when objects look and still lifes begin to live a remarkable life.

With the young of whom I speak, the human gaze rediscovers its rights. It burns and informs.

Right in the midst of this host of significant looks and objects which walk, right in the midst of this obedient rabble which attracts youth, a rabble against which for years I have been moving upstream, jostling with elbows and shoulders, right in the midst, I say, of this mythological rout, we saw Giorgio de Chirico release, in an artful manner, some frightening blind men.[29]

[29] In 1958 I still honor that young prince of disobedience who died because he wanted to see an Arab town which was like all the others, but forbidden. (Author's note.)

Colette

The friends Cocteau made when young remained his friends for life, although he was considerably saddened by losing some of them through premature death, Apollinaire in 1917, Radiguet in 1923 at the age of twenty, Erik Satie in 1925 when he was fifty-nine. Many of the people he described in Portraits-Souvenir were writers and actors whom he had admired from a distance when he himself was little more than a schoolboy. Yet one of these left the fin de siècle period far behind her and went through such far-reaching changes herself that her relationships with others changed too. This was none other than Colette, who was nearly twenty years older than Cocteau; he had observed her at the Palais de Glace, and made a drawing showing her flanked by her elderly first husband, Henri Gautier-Villars, known as "Willy," her bull-dog, and the brilliant young music-hall artist Polaire. Willy is only remembered now because without him Colette might probably never have written the Claudine books, or might never even have written at all. Polaire soon vanished from the scene; but Colette remained, a changing, perpetually deeper-seeing Colette, who gradually, almost imperceptibly became one of the greatest writers of twentieth-century France.

The early succès de scandale was not likely to have interested Cocteau very much, and he was in fact only a boy of eight when Claudine à l'École was published. At the same time Colette's originality had nothing to do with the avant-garde; it was as far away from it as Radiguet's return to classicism. Yet Cocteau was one of the first to appreciate Colette's mature writing; they became neighbors in the Palais-Royal and close friends, all the closer in fact because they had moved to the center of a circle from widely different points on the circumference. They were photographed and

Willy — Polaire
Toby chien et Colette au
palais de glace

Jean

*filmed together, and only the young and cruel could say that they
formed a mutual admiration society. When Colette's death in 1954
left her chair at the Belgian Academy of Literature vacant, it
seemed fitting that it should pass to Cocteau, all the more so perhaps because it had previously been occupied by his former friend
the Comtesse de Noailles. His speech at the official ceremony of
acceptance in Brussels contains an affectionate and perceptive picture of Colette, and contrasts vividly with the thumbnail sketches in*
Portraits-Souvenir, *which describe* "a thin, thin Colette, a sort of
little fox dressed up for cycling, a fox terrier in skirts, with a black
patch of hair over one eye, drawn up towards her forehead with a
bow of red ribbon."

*Even on this official occasion Cocteau was not much concerned
with literary analysis or "puffs." He did not say, as he did of
Apollinaire or Modigliani, that he would leave the critical judgments to someone else. He spoke of Colette the woman, the person,
for this is what he primarily valued—knowing that one does not
separate the creator from the creation.*

*Cocteau's speech is not given in its entirety here since he
quoted within it his earlier descriptions (from* Portraits-Souvenir)
of the Comtesse de Noailles. (See p. 13 in this collection.)

Two academic chairs, one in France and one in Belgium, are
almost too many for one man, particularly for one who normally
spends his life standing up. And the Belgian chair has been occupied
by two famous women. One of them had genius and to spare, and
wasted it. The other had a bursting money box and knew wonderfully well how to draw the money out. The first was a perpetual
invalid. The second became one, after having been a fox terrier
with indefatigable legs and a brown patch over one eye. When I
was young I passed many evenings at the first woman's bedside,
and when I was not so young, at the bedside of the second. This is
my excuse for accepting your offer to occupy this dangerous
place. . . .

Now I am in the Comtesse de Noailles' bedroom, in the rue
Scheffer. "Come in, dear Jean, I'm dead tired. Forgive me, I can't
say a word. I'll listen to you." And then, as Baudelaire used to say

of Victor Hugo, in Brussels, the Comtesse would plunge into one of those monologues that she used to call conversation.

And now I am in Colette's bedroom in the Palais-Royal. "Don't be afraid of these hillocks, they're my feet. Sit on the bottom of the bed. Do you want Pauline to bring you some food? Anything to drink? Are you thirsty? Are you hungry?" "No, Colette, I only want you." And Colette would go on with her embroidery and say "Have a rest, you don't know how to do nothing. You're no good at being lazy. . . ."

Do you recall a waltz that was famous in 1900?

En vain dans mes yeux distraits
Tu cherches à lire en moi-même,
Tu voudrais savoir si je t'aime,
Mais tu ne le sauras jamais.

These words were successful because they express the policy of women who make men believe they are in love when they are not and, when they are in love, keep it secret. This is where Colette, contrary to appearances, revealed herself to be more feminine than the Comtesse de Noailles. Anna classed herself with men and would never have condescended to do needlework. This deprived her of several secret weapons and turned her into a *tricoteuse*, one of those women in whose hands the knitting needle becomes a pike-staff. And you will not be surprised that I use such comparisons when speaking of the Palais-Royal, which was the scene of such spectacles. But behind the window where her blue lamp shone, Colette would never have wished, under any pretext, to join those women in the cruel garden below, who carried the heads of the guillotined. She hated children to play at war or crime. She hated that kind of heroism which, like alcohol, intoxicates men. After many escapades when she danced in the nude or traded in beauty secrets, she quickly returned to the fold. As the perfect daughter of Sido and the perfect mother of Belgazou, she cooked, gardened, waited for her husband to come home, rearranged the furniture and looked after the menu. You can guess what I want to say. It would be a little naïve to follow the parallel of the bravura piece—"The Comtesse wooed fame and fame eluded her. Colette spurned fame and fame pursued her." That would be too easy. Colette did not spurn fame. But she was clever enough to adopt the method described in our famous waltz: *"Non tu ne sauras jamais."* She lived as though fame did not exist. Fame fell into the trap, and whereas the Comtesse, who worshipped it so much, saw herself cruelly and unjustly abandoned, Colette made fame her slave, by a trick which is only a trick inasmuch as all women who are deeply feminine make use of it. . . .

1900. Each one of us has his own dates. For instance, November 11, 1918, for me, does not stand for the Armistice, but for the death of Apollinaire. It was in his honor that Paris put out flags. And as far as I am concerned, 1900 will always be that terrible year, the year Nietzsche died. But on the whole it is that feminine era when the woman of Paris dominated the monumental gateway to the Universal Exhibition and seemed to hatch out its art under her skirts. Naked women bestrode the steeds around the Grand Palais and led them by the bridle. A wave of Russian and German sensibility reached us from Dostoevski and Wagner. It was from Japan that another wave came, which under the label of Impressionism opened the windows of our naturalist, Cartesian France. In fact everything was ready for a young girl to arrive, hopping on one leg, from the country, to risk a break with convention and put out her tongue at Baronne Staffe and the Comtesse de Ségur; for a girl from Burgundy to hear under the enchanted tree voices which told her to go to the city; in short, since this is not Jeanette but Colette, everything was ready for a fresh tomato thrown from the gods to the stage to spatter the gowns of Paul Bourget's or Paul Hervieu's elegant heroines.

And then, many years later, there was a mysterious woman whom I was to know through her son, a fellow student at M. Dietz's establishment; a woman whom Edouard Bourdet made into the invisible Arlésienne in his play *La Prisonnière*, a woman whom one of the characters in the play honored with the brief remark "She never lies"; a woman whose nobility was such that under the name of Rézy she never forced Colette to find excuses for her; she announced all the characters who were to follow, characters whose spiritual level was enough for Colette to absolve them.

And then there was an old Parisian joker who, under the name of *L'Ouvreuse* and the halo of a strange top hat, knew, we might say, about music. He had no objection to directing the hand that threw the tomato, and like a bomb he dropped our little peasant girl, with her feet tied together, into the drawing-rooms which had been so unsettled by the Dreyfus affair that they paid no attention to literature and were prevented from being on their guard. . . .

In the Palais-Royal, where Colette knew me and transmitted her authority to me, we are a province, a kind of village haunted by the specters of the Revolution and the Directoire. I live in the apartment where Barras invented Bonaparte, and the sight of the wig-maker near the Comédie Française putting out his wax heads to dry on the railings around our garden evokes with terrible realism those newly severed heads which the sans-culottes carried there on their pikestaffs. And I have already told you that the children play at war and crime there, and that Colette detested these games. She would always put out her tongue and give a disapproving glance at the window, closing it to shut out the sound of toy-pistol shots.

That Palais-Royal, whose inhabitants when they climb the few steps to the rue de Richelieu say "I'm going up to Paris," had chosen Colette as its president, and after her death transferred to me its need for autonomy and its desire to group itself around a chief.

In the center of the village, the corner of the rue Montpensier, where I live, and the rue de Beaujolais, where Colette lived, stands the restaurant Véfour, which is directed by Monsieur Oliver. At the bar, at the hour when the little cannon in the garden used to thunder, raising a silky gust of pigeons like those in the Piazza San Marco, it has always been the custom for a few natives to meet and enjoy a drink together.

As soon as Colette expressed the wish to leave her chaise longue, at a sign from Monsieur Oliver two sturdy kitchen hands took up a kind of sedan chair and came down from the second floor with the President, who wished either to enter her car or go to a table bearing her name, which added luster to a place where many great men of France, from Fragonard to Balzac, were guests.

Unlike dictators, who are nearly always vegetarian and eat men, Colette liked good cooking, and her style proves it. Her style is heady, spares the salt and avoids fat, uses pepper, garlic and various herbs, and is not afraid of letting you bite a raw little red pimento, one of those little gnome-hats, which burn your mouth. . . .

A little wooden bridge formed her writing desk. Like certain big rivers she seemed to flow beneath it without moving. The current consisted of sheets, shawls and the sea-swell of the legs, which she didn't know where to put in her efforts to feel less pain. Day after day, just as in the past I had seen the fighting body of the Comtesse de Noailles struggle with death and rise from the sheets in her efforts to conquer it, I saw Colette flow quietly towards hers, beneath this little bridge, on which, like the Rialto or the Florentine archway, there would grow a heap of graceful untidiness, fruit, flowers, a bouquet of pens and a mountain of paper in which she would lose her way, searching in vain for what she wanted to show us, calling her husband to help and mixing up the blue sheets of paper under the blue lamp,[1] which made the Palais-Royal ghosts say: "Let us go. Colette is working."

Between the dust-cloud of her hair and the scarf knotted around her neck, set in that triangular face with its pointed nose and its mouth like a circumflex accent, were eyes like those of a lioness at the zoo who becomes the audience instead of the show, watching those who watch her, with folded paws and a sovereign disdain.

This was the pensive wild-animal look which Colette reserved for the people who came and stood in front of her cage. Her invalid leg had built this cage around her; once the curiosity of these people was satisfied and they no longer knew what to say, the roles were reversed, and it was the lioness who threw them a few words and dainties to eat until Maurice Goudeket, husband and keeper, appeared and directed them towards the exit.

I was occasionally present at these ridiculous visits, when vigil had been relaxed in Maurice's absence. Nothing was more comical than Colette's amiable purring, combined with her furious fingers

[1] The famous "Fanal bleu," which gave its name to a collection of essays published in 1949.

on the handle of her stick and the way she looked at me, like a drowning woman calling for help.

When we were alone everything changed. Her eyes lit up. Her curves became points. A strange mechanism came into operation, for in order to focus properly Colette's vision needed a great distance. She was inexhaustible on the subject of the Claudine period and seemed to be unaware of our own age, or else she attached no importance to it. But since this attitude was never accompanied by the slightest sign of intellectual fatigue and made no difference to the liveliness of her images, one had the impression that Colette refused to make decisions unless she stood at this indispensable distance and forced her mind's eye to obey the laws of perspective. For she was not content with recollection. She compared, pronounced judgment and weighed things up, and I have heard her make astounding remarks about Bayreuth, Mallarmé and Verlaine, the equal of which I have never encountered elsewhere.

I insist strongly, and I can never insist enough, on the fact that the greatness of Colette is due to an inability to distinguish between good and evil which placed her in a state of innocence; it would be unworthy to substitute for this a voluntary, artificial and conventional purity totally unrelated to the terrifying purity of nature, which men destroy by the disorder of their own order and the ridiculous verdicts of their own law courts.

I have seen Colette in pain yet refuse to take aspirins as though they were the devil's own pills, demanding that there should occur within herself, without any assistance, the mysterious mixtures and dosages of herbs and simples which the synthetic reconstitution of science can perhaps imitate, but only superficially and without recreating their virtues.

Let us honor in Colette a sage who stopped her ears in order to shut out the siren's song and refused nothing of the rich corruption of life. Like a true countrywoman she sensed that everything in nature that seems topsy-turvy possesses a secret significance and that the slightest alteration to any figure entails fatal errors in the total. . . .

I admit, then, that I cannot confirm the picture that people want to create, of a woman born from a cabbage, unaware of

getting and spending and set in the margin of our terrible world
like a small flower in a flower bed. First of all it is important to
realize that this humble flower probably has its own thoughts, and
that its thoughts are perhaps different from what one might believe. Those accelerated films, which we believe to be in slow motion, have revealed that a garden engages in fierce struggles, erotic
gestures and murders; if the country priest, as he waters his flowers,
could observe all this at human tempo, he would take to his heels.

While admitting that Colette belongs to the animal and vegetable kingdom, it would be wrong to find a place for her in a fine,
brave, motionless universe in a false serenity of nature whose extreme slowness of movement, in comparison to our own, caused
our innocent philosophers to be deceived for centuries on end.

Further, one should not confuse the protective cloud which
Colette maintained around her person, like the smoke screen around
warships, with the indifference of a spectator who is tired by the
spectacle and falls asleep. Liveliness never left Colette's mind and
there was no end to the curiosity she felt for every kind of thing,
big or small. "Maurice, look!" How often did we hear her say these
words in front of a plant or an insect.

The truth is that this plant or insect often came to take first
place. I think of Prince Andrew in Tolstoi's *War and Peace*, when
he was wounded on the battlefield. He looked at the clouds. All his
life he had dreamed of knowing his idol, Napoleon, and when he
heard the Emperor's voice as he approached, he did not even turn
his head to look at him. And I do not know whether the sudden
reappearance of Goethe or Shakespeare would have distracted
Colette from a spider spinning its web or from swallows attacking
a cat.

When I imagined that she was making inadequate contact
with problems which seemed at first sight to belong to her realm—
for example, Denis Saurat's researches on our insect ancestors—it
was not because I imagined her incapable of understanding them.
It was, on the contrary, because she was too near these phenomena
to study them; they were too closely related to her own substance
for her to observe them from the outside. If by chance I followed
my natural bent with Colette, forgetting her almost immodest
purity, if I so far forgot myself in her presence as to give, as it

were, stupid information to Clytemnestra or Electra on the behavior of the house of Atreus, Maurice, wearing the Egyptian
smile of the statues of Akhnaton, would appear as though by magic
through the curtains which separated the rooms; he heard me from
a distance, because Colette's slight deafness obliged me to raise my
voice. He would stand behind her where she lay, astonished,
frightened, convinced, ready to follow me, caught between her
devouring childish curiosity and the fear of upsetting her comfort,
and indulge in a whole pantomime of signs and gestures in order to
interrupt me.

Colette would raise her eyebrows, turn her head, catch sight
of Maurice, guess the type of scene that was taking place, and,
wisely renouncing the greediness which was beginning to triumph
over her diet, she would frown, her fine eyes looking from Maurice
to me and from me to Maurice. "Oh, Maurice," she would cry,
"did you hear? Listen! Come quickly, listen to what Jean's saying!
Be quick!" And without any transition she would close the door
into Bluebeard's cellar, which I had half opened, and through which
she had been irresistibly looking over my shoulder.

It might even happen that the danger would come from her
and that as she searched through her papers she would cry:
"Maurice! Where've we put the article about the children in that
Egyptian village who turn into cats at night? I must show it to
Jean, it was there yesterday on my table." And Maurice would
search without finding it, on purpose, and the curtain would fall
again in silence, and Colette retired again into her cloud, like a god
who knows more about things than we do, who was only taking a
polite interest in what we were saying, keeping up a pretense, in
order to hear us tell, for the first time, a very old story about
Mother Goose.

I remember wonderfully well my first meeting with Madame
de Noailles. But it would be impossible for me to remember how
or where I met Colette. In spite of my youth, and even because of
the wrong type of success that my personal *brio* earned me at that
time, that meeting with Madame de Noailles was theatrical and, to
use our modern terminology, spectacular. Whereas with Colette
that first contact seemed to count very little and happened more
surreptitiously, in the way habits are formed. I think she would

have found it as difficult as I do to recall the circumstances which made us seem like relatives who had lost sight of each other and then found each other again. What made it so easy for us to come together was the exchange of a host of memories about the social milieu where I was making my debut, and where she was already famous, without the intrigues of Paris ever bringing us face to face.

Since the shock of a meeting between a young poet and the Comtesse who reigned over the literary world at that time produced sparks, you can imagine what fireworks could be touched off by the meeting of the two women who, without knowing each other personally, shared between them the territories of verse and prose. And since this encounter took place when I already knew both of them, you can imagine that I have not forgotten it.

"We talked about the weather," the Comtesse liked to say, describing Colette's visit to see her on the fifth floor near the avenue Henri-Martin. And indeed it was remarkable how these ladies could have lived for so long in the same vegetable garden without meeting each other. But except on one of those clear evenings, when they can be seen together, it is very rare for the sun and moon to meet face to face. Who was the sun, you will ask, and who was the moon? I will award to Colette the role of the sun and to Anna de Noailles the role of the moon, which is the sun of statues and in one way the pale and cold sun of the dead, their glory, as La Rochefoucauld said. It was the moon's light that Anna de Noailles preferred to any other, and from it she drew her pallor, so different from the sunburn that Colette brought back from her holidays by the seaside.

I would like to conclude this speech with a few words of which you will not underestimate the importance. I read little. I re-read a great deal. But I do read, instinctively, whatever seems to me to reflect the preoccupation of the age. Most books of this type are written by women. But if their style shows an abandon which is the contemporary reply to precious writing, there is still a close resemblance between these works.

That inner eye, always at the service of a shameless sensibility or sensuality, freedom from all politeness and the formal dance of social life, a mania for truth at any price, even within untruth, a passion for describing oneself in minute detail and above all the

rehabilitation of idleness and disorder, for fear of obeying the hypo-
critical rules of bourgeois respectability, an incredible mixture of
sentimentality and filthy rubbish, these fragments of broken bottles
planted round the mind, this careless spitting, those cigarette ends
which remain alight beneath the heel that crushes them, those
sentences torn up from the depths with their roots, soil and all, the
declarations of love which consist of saying unpleasant things to
each other, that marshy iridescence like the Venetian canals where
cabbage stalks, orange peel and lovers' gondolas float along together—all that, extraordinary though it may seem, is the legacy
of Colette. This conclusion makes me think of the time when these
unusual combinations of words, and these images as juicy as fruit
and insolent as blows put us all on a regime of cold showers. We
were tempted to believe that boldness of this sort would soon cease
to be bold, would acquire the period charm of "modern style"
curves.

Embossed leather thistles, pokerwork irises, brass chestnut
leaves from Maxim's—these are the decorations we imagine on the
bed where Léa sips her chocolate and beaten egg yolks, watching
extremely severe elderly baronesses in impeccable dinner-jackets,
with cigars in the corner of their mouths, with very large feet and
hunting stocks, playing cards.

But we must not confuse a piece of furniture and the person
who paints it, Gauguin's armchair and the same chair painted by
Van Gogh, a concierge and the same concierge painted by Tou-
louse-Lautrec, a broom and Vermeer's painting of a broom. What
matters is not Léa's bed, but the fact that Colette paints it and
projects it outside fashion, space and time, that it collects our
wretched human mud and fashions iridescent soap bubbles from it,
that Colette's magic wand transforms an old trout into a fairy-tale
white cat and an alley-cat gigolo into that terrible wild creature
that Anglo-Indians used to call a golden cat.

And today, these books our ladies write, these American ball-
point pens which stain the pockets, these flames which leap out of
the cigarette lighter like devils, far from relegating Colette to the
shade, illuminate her with that light of which Violette Leduc
would say "Crudeness breaks into the room."

I must emphasize that there is no question of an accepted

influence, but of a certain atmosphere typical of two eras which are very different from each other yet more alike than one thinks. And I even remember saying jokingly to Simone de Beauvoir and also to Sartre, who did not contradict me, that *L'Invitée* was a kind of modern paraphrase of the age of *Claudine à Paris* and the *ménage à trois,* just in the same way as the swings in our fairgrounds resemble the swing in that delightful old photograph which shows Colette wearing long plaits and a straw hat.

But all the same, in Colette's immorality, and even because of that fresh innocence which constitutes its charm and transcends it, there lay the germ of that monstrous frankness with which our lady novelists mix the sexes. Colette was certainly the first who was not ashamed of her body, that maternal heap of entrails possessed by Rimbaud's sisters of charity and the *chercheuses de poux,* the first to model herself on nature and its countless attacks against modesty. Is she responsible for social disorder? No, and Goethe was right when he described the people who committed suicide after reading *Werther* as fools.

We should certainly honor in Colette the liberator of feminine psychology which had been caged by the scruples of the Princesse de Clèves and Madame de Chasteller, and certainly, when she renounced the pride which made these ladies value their virtue so highly, Colette made this virtue change places and opened horizons more subtle and vast than the rectangular canopy over a bed.

There is no need to whitewash Colette, because she is white. She disliked black as much as did the Impressionists, with whom she is in sympathy, although she never belonged to their group and was probably blindly indifferent to their researches. She is alone. Alone she was and alone she remains. And I emphasize this because strangely enough it was through belonging to no school and playing truant that she brought every school together.

Colette! She is here alive, among us, with bare feet and sandals, eating an onion from Saint-Tropez and calling: "Maurice, Maurice, can you hear what Jean's saying? Whatever will he say next? Listen, Maurice!" And I will ask your leave to be silent so that this strong voice can follow its course in your hearts, alone.

Al Brown

Diaghilev told Cocteau to surprise him, and Cocteau spent much of his life surprising others. In one of his last books, Le Cordon Ombilical, is a moving account of an unexpected personality in Cocteau's world—the Panamanian Al Brown, who held the world bantam-weight boxing title from 1929 to 1935 and later came to a sad end. In this description Cocteau transforms sport into a kind of theatrical magic and even boxers and their public become actors and poets.

. . . one of my adopted sons[1] is so foreign to the world of letters that he is almost a lyrical creation. I mean the former world bantam-weight boxing champion, Al Brown. The similarity between his methods and mine had struck me so forcibly that I formed the strange plan of bringing him out of his disastrous world of drugs and alcohol and proving, by putting him back in the ring, that intelligence, if used by a sportsman, is a weapon capable of replacing force. What is more, there was a kind of poetry in this colored man. This poetry exasperated the crowd, who despise it and scent it in all its forms. I enjoyed advising him and seeing him translate my moral struggles into the physical field. Al Brown, far from being handsome, radiated some indescribable kind of magic, and in the end the sporting crowds had to accept the mystery of his successes.

After a long and painful treatment, and in spite of the incredulous smiles of the professionals, Al Brown, listening to my advice, won eleven consecutive victories. I taught him how to win his adversaries' confidence by some childish tricks (for example: be-

---

[1] Cocteau is referring to the young men whose work he had encouraged.

fore the fight, drinking mineral water out of a champagne bottle) and, once the naïve athletes were on their guard, hitting them on the chin with the lightning speed of a cobra. It was his famous left hook which made Al Brown invincible, and unless he was tired after twelve rounds, letting himself appear to lose and winning the match on points. His method consisted of becoming a ghost, of never being where the pugilists thought him to be and only hitting them when he was quite sure of his blows.

How often did I see him disappoint the public by avoiding massacre! Whenever I except him from the family made famous by Raymond Radiguet, when I imagine the form of living death from which I took him and his end in Harlem, like that of a poor faithful animal going home to die in his kennel, I wonder whether all this strange enterprise is not a question of zombiism and whether it is not indispensable to add Al Brown to the list of my imaginary characters. Perhaps he died in Montmartre or during the terrible cure at Sainte-Anne, and I brought him back to life in accordance with the magic of voodoo. The fact remains that the pontiffs of boxing watched me during each match, for they were convinced that I exercised some hypnotic power over Al Brown and that from my place at the ringside I was conducting the fight. The referee had observed that the ex-world champion never took his eyes off me, and it is true that he would stroke his chin one second before knocking his opponent out, communicating to me by this sign that I could make bets with the journalists.

It goes without saying that I know nothing about voodoo ceremonies and that I have never attended any of their rites. I am unaware also of the credit that should be given to the zombies or whether they belong to reality or legend. But no legend comes into being lightly, and I would not dare to state that the macabre resurrectional phenomenon does not merit consideration. The methods of Al Brown, who was called the "Black Spider" or "Woolen Thread," were surprising because of their indifference to the rules, or at least to the recent ones of modern boxing, which the crowd want to be as spectacular as wrestling.

Al Brown respected the old rules of the noble art and, by means of a kind of dance, put his opponents off by preserving himself from blows and only administering those which he regarded as indispensable. He said that his fragile fists forced him to make feints likely to render himself invisible, and it is this skill in disappearing, when facing a colossus like Angelmann, which led managers to acquire a superstitious fear. I have heard him described as a "poet," a supreme insult which was aimed at me through him, and I have heard elegant women call out: "Kill him!" to young brutes who were astonished because they could never touch him. The final victory forced them to be silent and to seek the reasons for it in the inexplicable. Naturally it was easy to accuse him of sorcery and allege that he was only a puppet operated by me.

Steps were taken to forbid me to occupy a ringside seat, and on the evening when he was taken away on a stretcher, while the jury declared him to be the winner on points, I was afraid I would be lynched. He explained to me afterwards that San Chili had soaked his hair in a substance that induced drowsiness and that while hanging around his neck his one thought, after twelve rounds, was to beat him, mathematically, with the calculating blow of his left. On the evening of this match against the man who had used not very creditable means in the past to rob him of his title in Spain, specialists in good faith went so far as to allege that I had bribed the judges.

I presume, moreover, that Al was afraid of the risks involved in an organized encounter with a young English pugilist and was overtaken with childish fright; this is why he wanted me to write an article in which I was to state that the experiment was over and that I was withdrawing him from competition. The same press that had laughed at my attempt reproached me for bringing it to an end and for condemning "the black wonder" to the decadence of the Cirque Amar, with which he had just signed up to perform a number that was half-dancing, half-boxing, as he proceeded on his journey.

P.S. Cerdan, the day before his death, had promised me to take him under his protective wing. Al did not even have enough money to pay for a seat at his match. Knowing that he was very ill and that I had no time to go to New York, the journalists of *L'Equipe* made me record on tape my memories of a faithful friendship. Al Brown died in a Harlem hospital while listening to this tape.

Self-Portrait

In Le Cordon Ombilical *Cocteau wrote two paragraphs about himself making it quite clear that the secret of his personality was hard work. Otherwise, he adds, there is nothing to say.*

People have been looking for me for thirty years. The most important grievance fabricated by the witnesses for the prosecution in my Socratic trial is that I dissipate my efforts. Don't they know that an organism is made up of a heart, a liver, a gall bladder, lungs, kidneys, and so on? How could any creation live if it had only one organ? And what is more, they don't know that I never accept a task without tying it into a knot which can only be undone through the subterfuge used by Alexander. Cutting is not untying. But cutting advocates the method of winner take all, which is opposed to mine, that of loser take all. For the peasant-type lesson taught by Gordius was none other than a lesson in patience, given to an impatient prince who flew from triumph to triumph as far as this wretched boundary stone which he took to be the end of the world, a boundary stone on which he sat down and wondered: "What more can I hope for?" The oracle's reply: "A cigarette, a wristwatch, a racing car, a transistor, an airplane."

When people want to praise me they tell me I am a magician. A wave of the wand and the work falls from some heaven, ready-made, into my mouth. I am quite happy to tell them my secret: I work. I am a workman, an artisan, who perseveres and is not content with little, I admit. When I am locked inside the chapel at Villefranche like some pharaoh painting his own sarcophagus, I don't lose heart either by day or by night. I only go to bed when the wall speaks instead of me, and does not stammer. I give away the secret along with the method of using it. But people must know

Stravinsky, Diaghilev, Cocteau and Satie. By Larinov.

how to use it and the temptation to join the dancers and drinkers must not prevail. Sometimes I look at the dancers with envy. But I have accepted the tonsure, and even if I am trampled on, the wine I yield will only be stronger as a result, and if my cellars are emptied the Engadine and the specter of Nietzsche will fill them again. You will not find me. Get this sad certainty firmly into your head.